Emerging Approaches to Information Services

EDITED BY EDWARD BOWES

Head of events and books
Leah Darbyshire

Commissioning editor
Laura Slater

Editorial assistant
Edward Bowes

Published by ARK Group:

UK, Europe and Asia office
6–14 Underwood Street
London, N1 7JQ
United Kingdom
Tel: +44(0) 207 566 5792
publishing@ark-group.com

North America office
4408 N. Rockwood Drive, Suite 150
Peoria IL 61614
United States
Tel: +1 (309) 495 2853
publishingna@ark-group.com

www.ark-group.com

Printed in the United Kingdom by Ashford Colour Press Limited, Gosport, Hampshire

ISBN: 978-1-78358-294-5

A catalogue record for this book is available from the British Library

ARK Group is a division of Wilmington plc. The company is registered in England & Wales with company number 2931372 GB. Registered office: 6–14 Underwood Street, London N1 7JQ. VAT Number: GB 899 3725 51.

Contents

Executive summary

Over recent years we have witnessed a shift in the role of information services and research staff in law firms. These functions are in a period of transition, fueled by new disruptive technologies, increasingly competitive pricing, and building budgetary pressures. As law firms continually push to stay relevant in the digital age, the information functions will become less shackled to a physical library space and more widely implemented throughout the firm.

As law firms shift their work streams and cultures to align themselves with the digital world librarians, research staff, and knowledge managers will become more integrated in the firm's day to day functions, with more robust and powerful technology supporting them. With the wealth of data and new research potential this will open up, information services can now, more than ever, leverage a strong competitive advantage for law firms.

Emerging Approaches to Information Services sheds light on the shifting role of the information services function. With input from industry leaders from the libraries, research, and knowledge management fronts this title explores the best methods of optimizing the functions strategically. A range of methods for effectively utilizing a firm's resources are discussed; including integrating knowledge management (KM) and business development (BD) functions with library staff, realigning research models to avoid losses through unbilled associate hours, and the disruptive technology coming in to play (including upcoming independent research providers, awareness aggregation tools, and predictive analysis).

In Chapter 1 Constance Ard, information professional and consultant at Answer Maven, highlights how information resources and personnel can continue to prove themselves as valuable assets in a resource-constrained legal landscape. Addressing the need for library functions to translate their projects into solutions with firm-wide benefits, Ard explains that these functions need to shift to be a proactive, rather than reactive, service model.

Moving into Chapter 2 Mark Gediman, director of research services at Best Best & Krieger LLP, explores how a law firm library can effectively utilize knowledge management to help deal with partner requests. Using a real-world example of a request for a specialized repository of documents, Gediman runs through the key areas of information that KM has to offer, and how they can be leveraged to effectively respond to a partner's request.

In Chapter 3 Lance Sapsford, director of business development and marketing at Ince and Co, discusses how law firm libraries and information services can now play a role in driving growth and revenues. By combining three strategic elements, identified as knowledge, data, and digital resources, Sapsford highlights how capitalizing on these elements with an information services function can drive decision making and deliver revenues in the scenario of a change in legislation.

In Chapter 4 Michael Carrillo, business development and marketing manager, and Oz Benamram, chief knowledge officer at White and Case LLP discuss re-aligning a firm's research models to avoid losses that occur through unbilled associates hours spent on research. They suggest this can be done through a model involving embedded researchers – specialist information professionals who support lawyers in research tasks, freeing up billable hours. An embedded researcher model can be tailored to the firm's needs, to ensure that there is a best fit for the maximum impact.

Chapter 5 sees Annie Youngblood, manager of business intelligence for Pillsbury Winthrop Shaw Pittman, tackling an issue which is now critical for many law firms: how to capitalize on the shift towards competitive intelligence (CI) with a limited set of resources. The chapter outlines all the steps needed to launch an effective CI department: calculating the demand; finding appropriate staff; and pitching it to the workforce.

In Chapter 6 Marlene Gebauer, director of knowledge solutions at Greenberg Traurig, looks at the challenges that the traditional information services model faces, and how the system can be improved with the technological advancements in workflow automation. The benefits of mapping matters, identifying common request types, and creating delivery templates for greater ease of automation are discussed with examples ranging from litigation to onboarding lateral attorneys.

In Chapter 7 Steve Lastres, director of knowledge management services at Debevoise and Plimpton LLP, discusses the next step in content aggregation – content intelligence. Explaining that simply using content aggregation tools are not enough, Lastres delves into how firms can utilize their existing technology and professional expertise to move towards content intelligence, and doing so can leverage large amounts of unstructured data to make informed strategic decisions.

In Chapter 8 Jennifer Mendez, senior manager of KM firm solutions at Ogletree Deakins, discusses how artificial intelligence (AI) is transforming the way information professionals conduct research. The chapter is framed by a definition of AI and its upcoming role in law firms, then moves to explore how research giants Lexis and Westlaw are applying AI to create more efficient methods of research, along with smaller start-ups that are looking to disrupt the market.

In Chapter 9 Marica Burris, research and information services consultant at HBR Consulting, explores the evolving landscape of legal research providers – an aspect of law firm's information resources that are facing scrutiny from a budgeting and legal spend angle. In the content of shifting law firm value propositions, new entrants in the legal research providers have managed to gain traction – offering law firms a potential alternative to the standard, expensive platforms.

About the authors

Constance Ard is an information professional with nearly 20 years of library experience. She offers business information and content management solutions through her consulting practice Answer Maven. Before launching the consulting practice, Constance served as a law librarian for 12 years. She received her MSLIS from the University of Kentucky in 1995. Throughout her career, Constance has worked to develop a strong background in management and research as well as project management. She specializes in working with organizations to assess information problems, user needs, and expectations, and offers solutions to improve and leverage company expertise to solve those problems. This specialty includes working closely with management, end-users, and information technology. Technology and information are irrevocably intertwined and, in order to meet user requirements, information and content managers must work collaboratively with IT to ensure organizations meet their business goals. Constance is an expert at facilitating those relations. As a respected information professional, she has spoken on topics from legal research for non-legal researchers to e-Discovery preparation and big data text analytics. Constance served as the conference planning chair for the 2013 Association of Independent Information Professionals. She received the Outstanding Chapter Member Award from the Kentucky Chapter of Special Libraries Association in 2006 and the Professional Member Award in 2008. She also received the Kentucky Libraries Special Librarian of the Year Award in 2007.

Oz Benamram is the chief knowledge officer at White & Case LLP. Oz provides the firm with strategic direction on the use of KM and technology, and leads the knowledge department in developing and implementing the systems and processes that enable the firm to use its collective knowledge to benefit clients worldwide. Oz is a globally recognized thought leader and a frequent speaker on legal IT and KM subjects. He has won numerous awards for leading innovation in legal KM, including the creation of an enterprise search system.

Marcia Burris is a research and information services consultant at HBR Consulting. Marcia provides coaching and mentoring to librarians and information professionals to help them contribute high-value research and competitive intelligence services aligned with organizational needs, and builds effective and responsive research teams to add value to client service and positively impact firm performance.

Michael Carrillo is the business development and marketing manager for the Silicon Valley Office of White & Case LLP, where he helps to connect clients with beneficial legal services across practices and industries. His experience at White & Case includes working as a research and information services manager in the firm's knowledge department, a role that allowed him to develop needs based approaches to functions such as competitive intelligence and legal analytics. A native of Northern California, Michael holds a Master's of Library & Information Science from San Jose State University, and a BA in History from the University of California, Santa Cruz.

Marlene Gebauer is director of knowledge solutions at Greenberg Traurig. Marlene is an active author and presenter on legal research, training, knowledge management, and technology topics.

Mark Gediman is the director of information services for Best Best & Krieger, LLP and has been with BB&K since 2000, managing the research needs of more than 200 attorneys and paralegals in nine offi ces from DC to California. He is a past-president of the Southern California Association of Law Libraries (SCALL) and the co-founder and co-chair of the Competitive Intelligence Caucus of the Private Law Libraries-Information Professionals (PLL-IP) of the American Association of Law Libraries (AALL). He has over 25 years of experience in law library management and writes regularly on competitive intelligence, research, and library management issues. He presents frequently for AALL and the Inland Counties Association of Paralegals as well as for SCALL, NoCALL, ACI and HALL. He has authored Chapter 8 of *Business Intelligence for Law Firms* (ARK Group, 2012) and articles in *AALL Spectrum*, *Practicing Law Management Week*, *Paralegal Today*, and *Facts & Findings* – the magazine of the National Assoc. of Legal Assistants (NALA). He is a graduate of the University of California, Riverside.

Steve Lastres is director of knowledge management services for Debevoise & Plimpton LLP. He manages the firm's information and knowledge management initiatives with the assistance of a dedicated team of research, knowledge management, and technical services analysts. Steve works with a KM Task Force in charge of the firm's KM effort to develop and implement an effective KM strategy for the firm. He joined the firm in May 2005. Steve received a J.D. degree from New York Law School in 2003 where he received the Daniel Finkelstein Writing Award. He is a member of the Bars of New Jersey and New York. He received a Masters in Library Science with a Distinguished Achievement Award in Information and Library Science from Pratt Institute in 1996, and a undergraduate degree in Business Administration from Pace University. Prior to joining the firm, he was previously employed by the law firms of Arnold & Porter LLP and Fulbright & Jaworski LLP as a librarian and information and knowledge management professional.

Steve is active professionally having served as president of the Law Library Association of Greater NY (LLAGNY) and ARMA Metropolitan NY Chapter. He is past chair of the Private Law Libraries Special Interest Section (PLL SIS), member of the American Association of Law Libraries (AALL) Leadership and Nominations Committee and the ILTA Education Planning Committee, and former manager of the ARMA Northeast Region. Steve is also a prolific writer and speaker on the topics of KM and law librarianship. He was recognized as a FastCase 50 award winner which recognizes the top 50 innovators, techies, visionaries, and leaders. He was also an ILTA 2013 Publication Award Winner for Best Member-Contributed White Paper entitled "Knowledge Management: A Strategic Role Change for Legal Information Professionals" (http://epubs.iltanet.org/i/87421/32) and was recently awarded ILTA's 2014 Knowledge Management Professional of the Year Award.

Steve can be found on Twitter: @lastrst, and @privatelawLibs and Linkedin: http://www.linkedin.com/in/salastres.

Jennifer Mendez is senior manager of knowledge management firm solutions at Ogletree Deakins, a leading labor and employment law firm. In this role, she focuses on internal KM initiatives, such as ODConnect, the firm's award-winning SharePoint intranet portal, enterprise search, document automation, and other technologies to help streamline processes, as well as building and fostering a culture of knowledge sharing. She is also responsible for identifying, evaluating, and approving the purchase of research materials and electronic resources. Starting out as a law librarian Jennifer has implemented many tools for lawyers over the years, including research databases, SharePoint, enterprise search, custom development applications, and business development tools. She has a passion for delivering intuitive and accessible solutions.

Lance Sapsford is the director of business development and marketing at Ince and Co. Lance is responsible for all aspects of strategic and operational business development and marketing for Ince and Co globally. Lance has spent over two decades working in professional services, in corporate finance, consulting, and legal, with a focus on business development, sales, and strategic marketing.

Annie Youngblood is the manager of business intelligence for Pillsbury Winthrop Shaw Pittman. At Pillsbury, Annie is responsible for maintaining and growing the firm's business intelligence structure.

Prior to joining Pillsbury, Annie spent nearly a decade covering business and public policy on the local, state, and national levels for various news organizations. At the *Nashville Business Journal*, where she covered economic development and legal affairs, Annie was instrumental in spurring public debate about tax-payer money and corporate incentives. Previously a congressional reporter in Washington DC, Annie reported on the intricacies of the legislative and budgetary process. A native of Virginia, Annie also worked at various news outlets including the *Charlottesville Daily Progress*, *The Roanoke Times*, and the *Blue Ridge Business Journal*. In Roanoke, she was a weekly guest on an NPR affiliate where she hosted *Business Talk with Annie*.

In 2007, Annie was a stringer for *Time* magazine during the Virginia Tech shootings. She is a magna cum laude graduate of Randolph-Macon Woman's College in Lynchburg, VA, where she holds a bachelor's degree in economics.

Chapter 1:

Gaining a competitive advantage through corporate libraries and information professionals

By Constance Ard, information professional and consultant at Answer Maven

In any organization the most valuable assets are its personnel and its information. This is widely documented. In that context, it is surprising that, when economic crunches occur, the library is one of the first places scrutinized as a potential opportunity for cost reduction. It does not benefit businesses to be sentimental about their libraries. They need to be strategic and avoid being short-sighted. It is equally imperative for librarians to effectively serve the organization and communicate their value.

If both of these actions are taking place and the library is reviewed through the lens of long-range plans, potential contributions, and current value, the findings will most likely reveal both cost cutting opportunities and some investment prospects. Earlier this year, two law library blogs asked essentially the same question – what are we doing that we can stop?[1] This is an extremely strategic – and vital – question for a corporate library to take into consideration. Streamlining processes and discontinuing activities that do not support the organization's strategic vision is smart business.

What comes after this is the need to communicate the proactive actions that keep the corporate library a step ahead of what their user's need and want. If corporate librarians do not communicate their activities in a way that can be appreciated by the leadership, it makes it easier for those leaders to take a short-sighted view of the library.

Personnel and information as assets

Now that we have reiterated the importance of alignment with strategic vision, it is time to explore the concept of personnel and information as valuable assets within the organization. One way this is clear is because a lot of effort is placed on the task of retaining effective employees. Often, key employees will be given bonuses, salary bumps, and special benefits in an effort to retain them. Similarly, significant resources are expended to keep data secure in a company.

It is important to note that keeping data secure is only one aspect of maintaining and furthering its value. Being able to locate, "govern", and use information are imperative operations in today's workplace. A new term is surfacing to describe the landscape involved in handling organizational data: master data management (MDM).

Without the proper management of company information, sensitive information is lost or stolen.

MDM is a technology-enabled business discipline in which businesses and IT organizations work together to ensure the uniformity, accuracy, stewardship, semantic consistency, and accountability of the organization's official, shared master data assets. It is increasingly identified by organizations with the launch of a formal enterprise information management (EIM) strategy and the foundation of an information governance program that supports EIM.[2]

This use of a consultant created term does not significantly change the activities that have been present in organizations since the beginning. It just defines the concept in terms that reach beyond the network to include USB drives, mobile devices, and the security, governance, and management needed to keep information assets safe and accessible for the use of the organization yet out of the hands of the public.

Certainly "MDM" is an IT function. It is also an opportunity for the corporate library to apply information management expertise in a critical area of business. The separations between IT and IM are related to skills not responsibilities. Technology is imperative to delivering well-managed information. While the management is related to indexing, organization, and governance activities, the activities could not be executed efficiently without a strong and well maintained technology infrastructure.

Delivering services centered upon information in the company is a recognized value. The opportunity for increasing positive perception of the corporate library lies within what the service is and how it is delivered. Reports published over the past several years have highlighted the gap between what corporate leaders consider as critical library activities and services, and what the library is delivering. To be viewed and thus employed as a corporate secret weapon, the corporate librarian must up their game.

The recent Financial Times SLA report, "The evolving value of information management" actually contextualizes and defines the game plan by outlining the information related challenges of executives:[3]

- Information overload;
- Filtering located information;
- Identifying relevant information;
- Recognizing the currency of information; and
- Timeliness of retrieving the information.

With these specific challenges in mind, the corporate library must translate their projects into solutions that will address the executive's challenges. It is through this that the corporate library will retain and bolster support. This need to address the specific challenges recognized by executive leadership is forcing a review and revamp of existing models of library services. Librarians must think more analytically and change their deliverables.

Reaction and routine is out the door. So what if all of your users like you and qualify you as helpful? Unless those qualities assist in dealing with the timely use of the right information out of all of the available data, you are not answering the challenge of the executives. Now is the time to embrace innovation, creativity, and analytical capabilities to deliver services that matter.

James Matarrazo and Toby Pearlstein offer a valuable perspective on the need to be strategic and to move away from the reactive service model:[4]

"The most important asset that company librarians can bring is the recognition that aligning their services to the strategic goals of their employer will be the key to their success. In this manner the value of what they provide will be obvious because they will be part of the product of the organization as opposed to a service that is only tangentially aligned to the bottom line of their organization. The days of 'fetching' what your customer asks for and being reactive rather than proactive are long over; these now belong to Google, etc. The days of providing verifiable information where the librarians take responsibility for being an equal player in their organization's success are here. This will make information professionals a key asset to their funding unit rather than simply another service that can be easily marginalized and therefore eliminated."

Moving to a proactive model

The Australian Library Association discussion paper about the future of the library identified three themes that will guide professionals to that proactive model:[5]

- Convergence;
- Connections; and
- Golden Age of Information.

New models of services such as embedded librarians are contributing to the convergence and connection themes. As more and more companies change their own business models, opportunities are created for the information professionals to contribute to the work of the business in new ways.

According to the FT-SLA study, the new model seeks the application of basic information professional skills for proactive distillation and validation of information. Training is transforming into coaching and integration, with the company pushing the librarian out of their comfort zone. Justifying it all is the need to create measurements that focus on the company strategy rather than the muddled "library" metrics of old.

The performance gap will only be addressed by specific communication between information professionals and leadership about the shared understanding of the business and expressed needs to support it, the most useful result being the delivery of actionable information. In addition, the corporate library must communicate how their specific technical skills enable them to support the strategic initiatives of the organizations through their interaction, management, and delivery of usable information. Analysis of data is more important than ever. Remember the themes of volume, velocity, and variety. Those three influencers are creating a perfect storm for librarians to apply their skill set in new environments to go beyond ready reference and resource retrieval to recommendation, referral, and synthesis activities.

The current rhetoric surrounding the value of the corporate library is a broken record that has been playing for the past 30 years. The definition of the new model of valuable library service is evolving. The new options, the shifting technology, and the expectation of applied analysis is forcing a change in tune that deserves a chance to be heard.

The author sought input from the following LinkedIn discussion groups: SLA, information knowledge and content management. The responses indicated that the information professionals knew the time for outreach, strategic alignment, and identifying new areas in which to deliver services had arrived. The end users that participated in the discussion underscored the assumptions presented by the information professionals:

"Building Information Mining Tools is a great idea. I am not a librarian but consume a lot of information as a product manager. So I will come from a slightly different angle."

"Different groups in organizations have different needs. A corporate librarian can be a good source of aggregating various information sources (low velocity to high velocity information) and creating specialized streams for different functions sales, marketing, business development, product management and strategy groups."

"Librarians understand information, searches, ontologies lot better than their consumers. So they can provide a framework for information flows as well."[6]

The challenge presented to today's corporate libraries is to use their skills and the daily work activities to deliver aggregated, actionable information in innovative ways. This is what users expect and what executives value.

The technical tools and the information resources needed to deliver that information require care and feeding. While that may be a majority of the behind the scenes work that is performed in a corporate library, it is not what is currently valued. In other words, do not rely upon the explanations of the "black box" to support your value proposition.

Very few people want to know how things work when they are using the end product; they just want it to work. The competitive advantage for the corporate library is to apply their expertise to the challenge of making information work. Budget constraints, rising cost of collecting information, and the challenge of selecting the best technical solution for delivering the end result cannot be ignored, but they must not be the only thing mentioned when reporting upon the activities and importance of a corporate library. Shift the conversation to practical applications of those activities and you will address the challenges identified by your executives.

For example; "leadership's support of the investment in our upgrade to the electronic resource management system allowed the library staff to deliver three specific reports that addressed [XX] information need. The result was that the [analyst, scientist, technician] quickly verified the point of fact and was able to apply the information."

In short, stop talking exclusively in library-speak and use the skills you have to talk the talk of the company. Marydee Ojala and Ulla de Stricker have offered valuable guidance in how to partner, collaborate, and communicate within your organization. Apply that guidance, speak to the defined challenges, and be professional. Stop reacting and be the proactive leader in defining the opportunities that library services can create and support to deliver the competitive advantage. This will allow you as the information professional to reign supreme in the predicted golden age of information.

It is the duty of the information professional to demonstrate excellence in today's evolving corporate library landscape, as it nests within the larger context of the world.

References

1. See: www.geeklawblog.com/; http://deweybstrategic.blogspot.com/.
2. See: www.eweek.com/c/a/IT-Management/Master-Data-Management-Critical-to-Effective-Information-Governance-Gartner-276808/.
3. "The evolving value of information management", *Financial Times and SLA*, November 2013.
4. Interview answers prepared by Toby Pearlstein and Jim Matarazzo, January 24, 2014.
5. "Library and Information Services: The Future of the Profession Themes and Scenarios", Discussion Paper, Australia Library and Information Association, May 1, 2013.
6. Thodla, D., Response to LinkedIn discussion topic in the SLA group, February 6, 2014.

Chapter 2:
Library and knowledge management – A good fit

By Mark Gediman, director of research services at Best Best and Krieger LLP

One morning, in the not too distant past, I received an email from a partner with a question: Could the library help him to create a specialized repository for specific documents from a select group of clients that would be easy to access? This is the very definition of knowledge management: making the information the individual needs to access available in the most intuitive way possible. I'll talk about the steps involved in making this happen a bit further into the chapter.

Law firm knowledge management usually encompasses information contained in the following areas:

- Document management systems;
- Records management systems;
- Legal research;
- Training and professional development;
- Litigation support including eDiscovery processes and procedures;
- Client-facing products; and
- Matter budgeting and alternative fee arrangements.

Document management systems

First, the information contained in the documents and records management systems are commonly referred to as the firm's "work product". Let's focus first on the document management system, commonly referred to as the DMS. The majority of these documents are produced as a result of, or related to, specific client projects and matters. As a result, these documents usually count in the millions and may date back to the early days of these systems, stretching back 20 years or more. This makes determining and compiling the best documents based on different needs difficult. It isn't very efficient to have attorneys spend hours, if not days or weeks, reviewing documents to create topical document repositories. This is an area where the librarian's skills in search and taxonomy can be very valuable.

Although you may be familiar with the term "Taxonomy," it may be useful to review a quick definition. Merriam-Webster defines the term as:

> *classification; especially: orderly classification of plants and animals according to their presumed natural relationships.*
>
> (Source: https://www.merriam-webster.com/dictionary/taxonomy)

In a library, this term is typically used to identify a method of organizing information using short descriptive terms or codes. These taxonomies can be applied using terms from various sources. One commonly used taxonomy system is the Library of Congress Subject Headings (http://id.loc.gov/authorities/subjects.html). This system has existed since 1898 and, through many updates, remains an excellent source of classification of many types of information. However, it does have some drawbacks when attempting to apply it to information in a law firm context. For example, the term "civil discovery" is not included in this list. Also missing are "amicus," "wage and hour", and "mandamus."

Other taxonomy tools exist that have more relevance to the legal field. These tools include treatise table of contents, tagging, searchable document annotations, and standardized headnotes. An excellent example of a headnote classification resource is *West's Analysis of American Law*, 2016 ed. (Thomson Reuters). As described by the publisher:

> *West's Analysis of American Law is a complete guide to the West Key Number System, which organizes American case law into more than 400 main topics and over 100,000 individual lines.*

The key number system will provide standard terms for just about any topic covered in a law firm. This will provide a consistent structure and confidence that the terms will be widely recognized by the legal staff. If you have the companion West KM product, an integrated search tool automatically applies the key number to internal documents.

Tagging and annotating documents are features offered by some search engines, such as Lexis Search Advantage. This allows the flexibility of including topical terms, such as those taken from the table of contents of a specific practice's basic treatises and organizing the documents into a structure similar to that laid out in that table of contents. Using the table of contents to create a document tagging system allows for a structure tailored to the specific needs of the firm using terms from a resource they use regularly. For example, *California Tort Guide* (2017, CEB) includes a section on Premises Liability. In this section, the main headings are listed as follows:

1. Ordinary Care Standard (Rowland v Christian) 10.3
2. Effect of Visitor's Status 10.4
3. Owner's Conduct; Active Operations 10.5
4. Owner's Liability for Others' Conduct

This system gives clear and concise terminology as well as a method for organizing the file structure of the best practice database for this specialized area of law.

The challenge of determining best practice documents without involving the attorneys in the early stages can be daunting. This is especially true because the process of determining a best practice document can be extremely subjective. One attorney's favorite document may not be considered to be all that great by another. The other problem is the issue of having the attorneys invest their valuable time in this potentially tedious, non-billable activity. This can make implementing a knowledge management system for these types of documents challenging to say the least.

One possible solution to this problem is to look at document activity counts. Most search engines for document management systems include the ability to view the activity or views received for each document in the system. A reasonable assumption, at least for the initial filtering stages, is that the documents with the high number of views are perceived as best practice documents. Using this data point can significantly reduce the number of documents that would need to be reviewed for inclusion in the best practice collection. Quantifying what can be a subjective process is another advantage of this process.

Records management systems

Records management systems are not much different than document management systems. In fact, some classify document management systems as a type of records management system. However, the term "records management system" usually refers to the system used to track the hard copy client files of the firm. The knowledge management aspect of this is again the ability to find what the legal staff needs in a quick and intuitive manner. The librarian's unique knowledge of search techniques and how the attorneys work can make a difference in creating a useful system. The basics seem simple: type a client-matter number and view the records for the desired file. And it can be simple. In order to accomplish this simplicity, it is necessary to look at how results of this research are displayed. Providing too much information, such as listing out subfolders by default instead providing a clear view with the option to drill deeper into the file structure will unnecessarily complicate the ability to find the needed file. Less is the goal here, without omitting important pieces of information such as retention dates and privacy restrictions.

Legal research

Legal research is one of the lesser known aspects of knowledge management. Hundreds of searches are run each month by library staff, attorneys, and paralegals. The details of these searches, including search techniques, lessons learned while conducting the research, and the resources found during the research are important information to not only the research professional but for the firm as well.

A common tool used to capture information on search techniques and lessons learned is a knowledge base. A knowledge base is organized along the lines of a traditional database and can be linked to the record of the original request in a library team management system such as Reference Tracker (eos), Quest, Quatrove, or Sydney Plus to retain information related to specific research requests. These databases can be purchased as an add-on component for the library management systems referenced above or created using the firms document management system with an excel spreadsheet to record the original requests. Librarians can use this system to record their research methodology for difficult research projects and share knowledge with others to provide a guide for this type of research project.

Research projects often find items that can have value to others in the firm aside from the individual(s) that originated the project. The type of items with value beyond the initial research project include but are not limited to maps, government reports, and studies. The goal is to make them accessible to anyone at any time who find they need to review them during the course of their research. Here are a couple of simple cost-effective solutions:

1. In the document management system, create a client matter number specifically to house these documents. Then create topical subfolders and organize the documents accordingly.
2. Add these items to the catalog in your library management system and organize the information along the same lines as other library materials.

Training and professional development

Training and professional development materials are typically items that are overlooked when examining the scope of the knowledge management system. These items are usually compartmentalized by department and are not organized topically. Rather, the default organizational scheme is usually based on the CLE requirement met, practice group who requested the professional development resource or the type of administrative skill being taught. However, these items lend themselves very nicely to the taxonomy structures discussed above. A program purchased for the Real Estate Practice Group can be classified according to Premises Liability instead of being grouped together with programs on Sales Contracts and Deed of Trusts. Similarly, administrative training programs on creating a Table of Authorities can be tagged as a pleading or litigation process instead of being grouped with all of the training programs related to Microsoft Word.

Litigation support and eDiscovery databases

Litigation support and eDiscovery databases are often separate from the firm's document management systems and don't often receive the same attention as the more mainstream document repositories when it comes to applying the firm wide organizational structure. There may be some disagreement about whether or not these even should be considered. These databases are intended to manage large amounts of documents specific to a particular case so the organization of the documents are often dictated by the litigation. However, applying the firm's taxonomy to these documents can give the reviewing attorneys and paralegals a familiar basis and mechanism for researching documents in the databases that may aid the process of finding relevant documents.

Client-facing products

Many firms have set up extranets or accessible external websites that allow the attorneys to collaborate and share documents with the clients directly. Just as the internal repositories mentioned above, these websites are also subject to becoming unwieldy over time. This can create frustration on the part of both the client and the attorney. Organizing the documents using a taxonomy common to both parties can make the sharing of information more intuitive and less frustrating. The folder structure and language will necessarily differ from what is used within the firm because the firm's filing methodology may not be intuitively understood by the client due to their different frame of reference. This should be taken into consideration when creating a structure for the extranet.

Matter budgeting and alternative fee arrangements

Matter budgeting and alternative fee arrangements are based on the idea that the firm can streamline their handling of specific matter types to limit client costs while still showing a profit. A good knowledge management system makes it easier to leverage prior work products and experiences to efficiently perform the requested task. This removes the necessity for the attorney to "reinvent the wheel" each time this task is performed.

Now for the request I mentioned at the start of this chapter: Could the library create a specialized repository for specific documents from a select group of clients that would be easy to access?

To me, the most important part of this request is very last phrase: "easy to access."

Below is my step-by-step process for responding to this request.

Full disclosure: This process is using iManage and Lexis Search Advantage (LSA). Your experience may vary based on the resources in your firm.

- Create a specific client matter worksite in the document management system to house the documents. NOTE: Keep the folder structure minimal. I only use the document folder. It makes it easier to populate the database later on.
- The separate client matter worksite creates a location that is separate from the document management system. This location also makes it easier to create an intuitive retrieval process for these documents. More on this below.
- Search on the specific documents and rank by activity count.
- As mentioned above, this is one way to determine popularity and usefulness.
- Make a list of the documents with the larger counts.

- These will be the documents that will be part of the best practices file
- Copy these documents into the documents folder in the worksite.
- Run different searches and save the URL for each one.

NOTE: Limit each search with the following criteria:

- The specific client matter number for the worksite
- Use the specific document type
- Any unique terminology

LSA creates a fixed URL for each search session. It will automatically update the search with any documents that are added to the worksite each time the link is clicked.

- Add the URLs as links to the practice group.

The solution is just one of many ways that these can be set up. For instance, these documents could be tagged with standard terms that will allow them to be easily included in other searches run in the document management system. The idea was that every step would result in a system that was simple to update and simple to use. The less time spent searching for specific types of documents results in a more efficient process and less frustration by the attorneys.

Conclusion

One question I often get asked is should librarians be involved in knowledge management? My answer? Duh! Librarians have the skills and knowledge necessary to make any knowledge management program a success. The primary function of any librarian is to maintain and organize knowledge in way that preserves it while simultaneously makes it accessible. Librarians know the culture of the firm and have the frame of reference to tailor the knowledge retrieval process to the specific needs of the firm. The research skills of the librarian are essential in understanding how to organize the information so it can found easily by non-library staff. This chapter has shown how the unique ability of librarians to organize information and understand how the end user looks for that information can make a knowledge management program successful.

Chapter 3:
The role of the law firm library in driving growth and revenues

By Lance Sapsford, director of business development and marketing at Ince and Co

UK Law firms have evolved over many years and they have done so almost solely with the law in mind. The fact that they are generally very profitable has been a perk of the job that comes with traditionally high barriers to entry. The reason for making these points is that times have changed in three specific areas – knowledge and intellectual property, the use of data, and the advent of digital capability of all types. These changes offer opportunities – the law firm able to take full advantage of and adapt to all three of them stands to gain significant competitive advantage.

KM functions (usually backed up by an information or library service) traditionally exist to inform lawyers and clients about developments in the law. They do not necessarily interpret the law for the benefit of clients. Perhaps the most common complaint of in-house teams regarding law firm suppliers is "tell me what I need to do; don't tell me what the law says".

Changes to the amount and nature of the data law firms produce or have access to have developed hand in hand with the use of technology. What hasn't changed greatly is how this data is viewed and used in law firms. Big data as a concept is well established and has already had a major impact on all our lives – its true power is only just being realized as computer power, storage and speed continue to grow. Law firms do not necessarily recognize or prioritize the analysis of the valuable information at their command as it does not readily fit with the way law firms are structured or operate both on the legal and business services sides.

The digital world has seen the most significant changes. The computer power at our fingertips able to manipulate data and deliver us actionable intelligence is now enormous. The web is now a sophisticated marketing, sales, and information delivery tool; our ability to analyze, layer, and interpret information has advanced in ways it was impossible to predict even 10 years ago. Email traffic, mobile access, cloud based services – the list goes on – are all underutilized by law firms.

In addition, the three elements above are certainly not co-ordinated in many (if not most) firms.

What can be done to capitalize?

The answer to this lies in understanding the relationships between knowledge, data, and digital as it applies to law firms. It is the power of all three of these elements, when used well together, which is waiting to be unlocked.

If we accept that a law firm is there to assist its clients to achieve their goals through the delivery of legal services, then how can firms use their IP, the data they could collect, and the power of digital to a) understand what their clients are concerned with now and in the future (something needed to help them achieve those goals), b) use this insight to make business development, marketing, and client relationship decisions, and c) create a pipeline of business of the right type to sustain the levels of profitability to which they have become accustomed?

Some definitions and a bit of context

Knowledge: After centuries of development the law is complex. It is that complexity which has given rise to a regulated industry there to assist in providing guidance through the legal landscape to individuals and clients alike. This, in turn has created barriers to entry (exams are required, registration must be adhered to, and practicing certificates maintained). This has concentrated expertise in the hands of law firms who, as a result, can dispense advice on the law at a premium. And at the centre of all this is the expertise upon which the advice is based – the knowledge.

In marketing and business development terms, this knowledge can also be used to create revenues through thought leadership – opinion and interpretation of the law as applied to situations of interest to clients without the technical expertise (or the scale or budgets to pay to have it) in-house. It is here that the real value lies – the use of this scarce knowledge to inform client decision making, help them avoid or mitigate risk, get one over the competition, and so on. An extreme manifestation of this is that of US firms creating their own, large scale litigation – class actions around a researched transgression which a firm uses to bring enough claimants together to fight a case that would not otherwise be fought – and all based on their knowledge of the law and its application to a commercial situation.

Data: Data has multiple sources in all firms. Finance, CRM, email marketing systems, websites, events statistics to name some of the obvious ones. The types of information available are many and varied – click through rates to articles and updates; financials on individual service lines or clients; web analytics, user journeys, visitor identities, numbers of page views; attendance rates, response rates, new matters; conflicts information; win rates for different types of pitches – the list is long. Combining these data sets to create actionable intelligence and to inform decision making can be done in many ways. Currently most firms look at single source of data and do so in isolation. Examples of how this "data layering" can work are given later.

Digital: Computing power – our ability to crunch data – is nowadays not expensive and is easily accessed. The internet is a first port of call for almost everything; search is incredibly sophisticated – it supports a whole industry in its own right. Digital is the future – it offers competitive advantage to those who come up with the best ways of using it and creates wealth along the way. Most law firms are, for the most part, still using the internet as a platform for an online brochure.

So how can these three elements – knowledge, data, and digital and be combined to drive decision making, create opportunities and ultimately deliver revenues? There is no single answer to this but a simple example might help. Let's take a change in legislation – say the General Data Protection Regulation which will come into force in May 2018. We know the date that the legislation will take effect (or at least begin to be policed) and we also know that clients will need to be compliant at that point. As shown in the diagram below it stands to reason that the attention of in house lawyers responsible for ensuring their businesses aren't fined as a result of non-compliance, will turn their attention to this as a project as it approaches. The time to position a firm to benefit from the legal work that will flow from this change starts now and involves profile raising, marketing, and awareness. As the legislation gets nearer, marketing activity turns to BD and sales activity and ultimately to a pitch, or, even better, direct instructions.

But how can a firm know who is interested and where the likely buyers are? Data is the key. Using knowledge as the hook (GDPR expertise), data is thrown up from invitations to seminars, web visitors, click-throughs, prior attendances, and website analytics as client interest increases over time. Capturing this data which comes from multiple sources (all digital in some way) and using it to inform which clients are buyers then planning appropriate marketing and sales activity is the next stage. Put simply, law firms have the knowledge clients want – they can use the

Sales Cycle – Combining Knowledge, Data and Digital

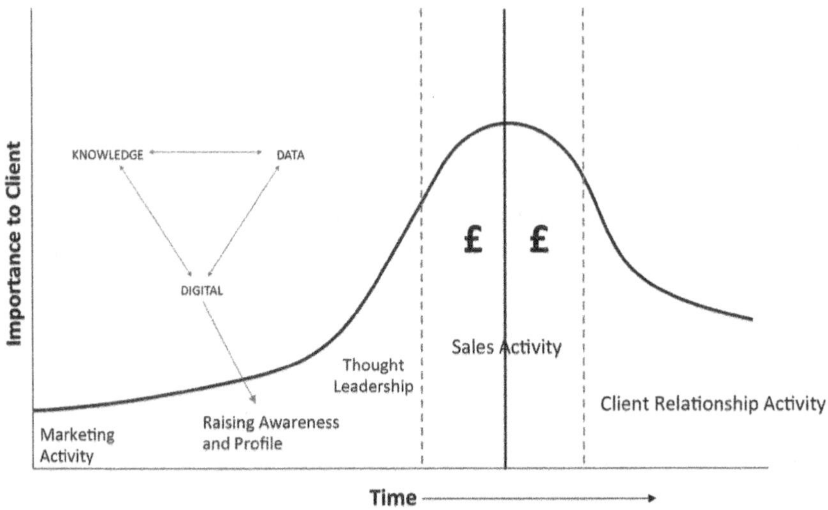

data they throw up to make decisions on how to go to market by using sophisticated digital tools to crunch the data.

A good source of data is the "long tail". Law is specialized and search is too. The less common or, to put it another way, the more specialized (longer and detailed) a search term, the greater the chance that a specialized firm will be able to capture those looking to understand a complex, knowledge based issue or need. In our case an in-house lawyer looking for an answer. If your site has the right content and you can see who's looking (within the data protection rules of course) the more highly qualified leads you will generate. You can effectively generate your own leads. This clearly demonstrates the value of well-planned SEO.

Bringing together all the sources of data, using digital technology to interpret that data and then making decisions based on the findings is the key. Other examples might be layering website traffic over service line revenues by client. If, for example, there is a lot of web traffic from one client on your website for a given service line and you do no work for them in this area – the opportunity to discuss this with the client service team is obvious. Conversely, if there is no traffic to your website but you do a lot of work for them in this area, a conversation with the digital marketing team (including those who deliver content) may be needed – you're probably missing a trick and missing out on new business from other clients as your content is either not good enough or is not well search optimized.

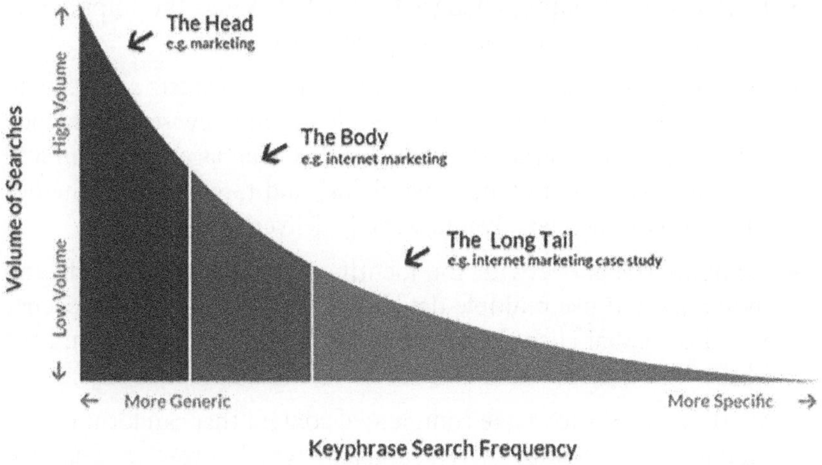

Layering a client's propensity to instruct (frequency and size of instruction) on top of all the different types of intervention your firm makes with them gives an interesting view of the effectiveness of your marketing, BD, and client management engagement. Finding that a target client attends seminars, uses your website regularly, and is an avid reader of your researched technical updates or knowledge bank but does not instruct you other than for one minor service line for example – what does this mean and how can it be addressed? Likewise finding that seminar visits regularly yield new instructions from a particular person by looking at the timelines of both together speaks for itself in terms of decision making.

Where does the library function fit in?

Firstly, most library functions have moved towards being information services functions. This is a logical step as online resources of a legal, technical nature are as easy to find given the right subscriptions as anything else. Why not combine legal research with more general business analysis on clients or markets, say?

The change that has not fully taken place yet is that of library/information functions going from a reactive stance to a more integrated, proactive one. By this I mean a function that is integrated with multiple areas of the business (not just the lawyers) and which understands what the BD, marketing, and sales priorities of the business are. Imagine a firm where partners opening new markets can tap into a library function that works with lawyers and business development professionals from across the firm to:

- Interpret forthcoming changes to legislation and the impact that these will have on individual or groups of clients;
- Use the insight gained to work with sector specialists and PSLs to develop marketing content, new products, and new services which can be taken to market through the client management team and new business programmes that clients and targets alike value for their the commercial advantages they deliver;
- Combine the above with the identification of market trends and dynamics and use multiple data sets to test and refine approaches based on actual client behaviours, SEO results, analytics, and the like;
- Work with PSLs to create commercial content that can form part of an integrated, digitally driven campaign which throws up qualified leads that the BD team and the partnership can act upon to deliver opportunities for revenue generation that the bids team can help to close;
- Take enquiries on cases or points of law and analyzes them for applicability to other clients or even sectors passing the results through to client teams to use as the basis for ongoing dialogue and ideas transfer in the nurturing of strong client relationship management; and
- Contribute to a marketing and BD action plan based on a timeline of legislative change the activities of which can be measured for return based on the revenues generated from the relevant products and services developed.

The future of business services in law firms lies in its ability to integrate both the separate and often silo-driven functions. At the heart of how a law firm delivers value to clients lies its legal knowledge – something for which the library is a guardian. The library function itself needs to recognize this pivotal role and to change its emphasis towards playing its part in commercializing that knowledge. The firm that establishes this kind of library function along with the integration that modern law firms should be striving for will be well on the way to realizing the full potential of the knowledge at its fingertips – combining such a function with the power of digital and the intelligent use of data is the Holy Grail.

Chapter 4:
Turning losses into gains – Realigning law firm research

By Michael Carrillo, business development and marketing manager, and Oz Benamram, chief knowledge officer at White and Case

How much revenue does your law firm lose every year on unbilled research?

A study published by the consultancy firm Blue Hill Research, reports that written-off associate research hours may reach over $60,000 per associate, per year.[1] In Big Law, where firms staff hundreds of associates, annual losses may run into the millions of dollars. A realigned research model gives firms an opportunity to improve their client service while turning losses into gains through the strategic use of embedded staff researchers.

Background

The financial crisis of 2008 unleashed unprecedented cost pressure on the legal sector as corporations increasingly demanded more for less from law firms.[2] As a consequence, the post-2008 legal industry is defined by fierce competition and internal budgetary austerity. Some clients now require their legal counsel to discount fees for research conducted by junior lawyers, or set these costs aside completely.

The Blue Hill Research study estimates the typical law firm associate spends 193.3 hours a year doing research that is written off client bills. Using the average of $320 an hour, this sum translates to $61,856 in unrealized annual revenue per associate. It's important to note that this study only considered associate time doing *legal* research. The lost revenue would be significantly higher if it included unbilled time spent on *non-legal* research.

From a business perspective, this trend is alarming. Research is inescapably necessary to the practice of law, but attorney salaries and subscriptions to high-priced information resources immediately turn into overhead when unbilled. Because losses of this magnitude have a meaningful impact on their bottom line, law firms should explore alternatives to absorbing research expenses as a price of doing business.

The business case for embedded researchers

Firms can improve performance by embedding researchers – also called law librarians, information professionals, or research analysts – within specific practice groups. As research is the primary focus of their work, embedded researchers are experts with the cutting-edge methods and tools necessary to perform this function. They know where the relevant information lives and how to get it, fast. In practice, this means dedicated researchers often provide *better results in less time* than associates. A research professional with three years of experience is significantly more proficient in this area than a third-year associate, whose time is fragmented between research and the other tasks required by the practice of law. If embedded researchers can do research faster than associates, or at least support associates in navigating the research process, they create efficiency, minimize wasted time, cut costs, and contribute positively to the firm's bottom line.

First, by reallocating otherwise unbillable research projects from associates to embedded researchers, associates are freed to focus on work aligned with their higher hourly rates. Thus, transitioning unbillable research from associates to staff researchers potentially enables firms to realize an additional $62K per associate in annual revenue.

Embedded researcher salaries are also lower than those paid to associates, so in the event their time gets written off, costs incurred by the firm are significantly reduced. Accordingly, firms can give clients more value, while taking less of a financial hit from research.

Staffing versatility in this context is especially important for firms transitioning from traditional bill-by-the-hour engagements to alternative fee arrangements, where fixed or flat fees are becoming the new norm.[3]

Additional overhead reductions can be recognized through cutting subscriptions to increasingly expensive information resources. If the research function is focused in a core group of research professionals, the need for costly enterprise licenses to certain research tools is eliminated. Of course, information resource vendors would undoubtedly push back on any effort to abridge current licensing agreements, but a decrease in demand would present a solid platform for contract renegotiation.

Essentially, in the current business climate, much can be gained through the use of embedded research professionals:

- Costs are reduced by increasing the speed and efficiency of the research process;
- Revenues per attorney are increased by maximizing the use of associates' time;
- Overhead is decreased, because researchers' salaries are lower than associates';
- Versatile staffing allows firms to pursue alternative fee arrangements; and
- Money is saved by reducing expensive information resources and including online databases and physical subscriptions.

Impact on attorney research skills

Just as many Big Law practitioners no longer spend hundreds of hours performing lower level tasks, such as document review, associates should not spend time doing research if this function can be pushed to less expensive, more qualified workers. When managed by practicing attorneys, document review has successfully been outsourced to third-party vendors or to in-firm legal support staff, such as paralegals or eDiscovery specialists. In the same way, staff researchers can take on much of the research function when overseen by legal practitioners. However, one fundamental difference between document review and research is that research has been considered core to the practice of law.[4]

Surveys suggest that newer attorneys spend between 30 percent and 60 percent of their time doing legal research[5] – a potentially important developmental task for junior associates whose long hours spent interacting with legal information may help them to gain a greater understanding of the law. Yet, legal professionals have noted the lack of legal research skills possessed by new attorneys, stating that these individuals "are unprepared to conduct legal research and that their research skills are unsophisticated."[6]

Though some may consider expanding the role of embedded researchers to come at the detriment of attorney development, law firms must decide whether it makes both professional and economic sense for junior associates to inefficiently dedicate their time to building their legal research skills, when they could be focusing more on legal analysis and strategy. Fortunately, the choice between associate or staff researcher does not have to be an "either/or" debate, where law firms are forced to decide between staff and attorney research.

Even where law firms draw heavily on the skills of research professionals, attorneys are never excluded from the process. Working alongside experienced researchers, new attorneys sharpen their research skillset. They also hone the collaborative and managerial skills that lead to career advancement. Moreover, despite the fact that professional researchers can expedite the research process, it is still incumbent upon the legal practitioner to analyze and apply the law to the facts of their particular matters. It is through the application of these strategic and analytical skills that attorneys create client value.

Collaborating closely with associates is also extremely helpful to embedded researchers, who are then able to tailor their research methods to the specific needs of the legal practitioner's strategy as it develops. In this way, research informs attorney strategy, and attorney strategy helps to focus subsequent research. Embedded researchers will never replace attorneys. Instead, researchers and attorneys have a symbiotic relationship, each making the other better at what they do.

A blended research model

Research remains an important aspect of the business of law; but, Big Law has now been challenged by New Law, and business models across the industry are changing to promote client value.[7] In this evolving economy, a staff researcher model should be used where not doing so endangers firms' abilities to competitively serve their clients.

The challenge here is the same balancing act facing all businesses operating in a market economy: earning profits while offering a reasonably-priced product. In context, deploying embedded researchers should aid in this process by competitively pricing research and allowing associates, the main law firm revenue generators, to appropriately focus their efforts. The key then becomes finding the right associate-to-researcher ratio that both maximizes client-value, and maintains firms' solvency.

Fortunately, the embedded research model can be tailored to each firm's needs, based on clients' attitudes towards research and the type of legal services being purchased. For instance, where clients feel that certain research is worth associate fees, a blend of associates and research professionals might work well. Here, research still helps to maximize associates' utilization, and client-value is created through discounted researcher rates.

In a second example where the client does not mandate associate research, embedded researchers can take on more or all of the research function. While the research revenues may be lower in this model, overall income has the potential to be higher when associates are able to use time normally written off for higher level activities.

Finally, where clients are unwilling to pay for research altogether, the use of staff researchers will substantially decrease overhead. Multiple staff researchers can be employed for the same salary as one junior associate, so it costs much less to have staff researchers do work that cannot be billed.[8] In the face of recent associate salary hikes, implementing a staff researcher model may actually become a business imperative necessary to avoid some of the pitfalls surrounding this pay increase.[9]

Salary is not the only consideration. Overhead associated with office space should also be calculated. Many firms report success with opening shared services centers in low-cost geographies to offset the price of doing business in expensive metropolitan hubs like New York or London.[10] Though not without its challenges, now that most research can be done using primarily electronic information resources, an embedded research model allows researchers to sit with the practice groups that they support instead of being tethered to the physical library. This gives firms the flexibility to further reduce the library footprint, and support certain operational functions at a lower price point via shared services centers.

This same technological evolution that has allowed research to expand beyond physical libraries will continue to shape the future of the legal industry at large. Machine learning, for instance, has revolutionized the process of eDiscovery, and its applicability to other aspects of legal practice should not be underestimated.[11] When thinking about an embedded research model, it is tempting to consider how technology might augment human researchers. However, there remains a big difference between answering relatively simple questions, such as "Can a bankrupt company still conduct business?" and researching the finer points of how judges in the Eastern District of Texas will construe means-plus-function claims in patents relating to video streaming methods.

Even as advances in artificial intelligence are made, taking advantage of the latest technological developments requires further expertise, which is easier to achieve within a small group of research experts than in a large associate population.

All of these evolving considerations make up the basis for a blended research model. While a changing economy and developing technologies create opportunities for innovative approaches to law firm research, it's important to recognize that these changes will not eclipse traditional methods of doing business, but rather, enhance them. There is always room for improvement, but this should not come at the expense of already exceptional client services.

Consequently, thoroughly assessing what works well is an indispensable first step for any firm contemplating an embedded research model. Pilot programs embedding researchers within specific practice groups can present a good method for determining correct researcher-to-associate proportions. These programs necessarily allow for the flexible implementation of a staff research model by degrees, and they can provide important metrics for evaluating success along the way. Change may be inevitable, but it can be managed intelligently to benefit clients and law firms alike.

High-value, right-priced service

Law firms need to conduct business similarly to their clients, anticipating and responding to market forces in order to stay competitive. Firms that are unable to adapt to these economic realities give clients every reason to buy legal services from competitors, or move legal work in-house.[12] A staff research model that balances staff and attorney expertise is one tactic law firms can pursue to keep their operations profitable and strategically ahead of the industry. Some firms may indeed have variations of a staff researcher model already in place, while others may have not considered this option. Though the circumstances of each firm will undoubtedly differ, using staff researchers to cut costs and expand attorney output is just good business.

References

1. Houlihan, D., "Calculating the Value of Legal Research Efficiency", Blue Hill Research (Aug. 29, 2014). See: http://bluehillresearch.com/calculating-the-value-of-legal-research-efficiency/.
2. Lamm, C., & Verrier, H., "Large law firms: A business model, a service ethic", in *THE RELEVANT LAWYER—REIMAGINING THE FUTURE OF THE LEGAL PROFESSION* (Paul A. Haskins, ed., 2015). See: http://www.whitecase.com/publications/article/large-law-firms-business-model-service-ethic.
3. Germaine, C., *Why Law Firms Should Be Eyeing Attorney Layoffs*, Law360 (Jul. 8, 2016). See: http://www.law360.com/articles/814729/why-law-firms-should-be-eyeing-attorney-layoffs.
4. Lastres, S., A., *Rebooting Legal Research in a Digital Age*, LLRX (Aug. 10, 2013). See: http://www.llrx.com/features/legalinstruction.htm.
5. See: LexisNexis, *White Paper: Hiring partners reveal new attorney readiness for real world practice* (2015). See: http://www.lexisnexis.com/documents/pdf/20150325064926_large.pdf.
6. Kaplanm A., B., & Darvil, K., *Think (and Practice) Like A Lawyer: Legal Research for the New Millennials*, 8 Legal Comm. & Rhetoric: JALWD 153, 155 (2011). See: http://www.alwd.org/lcr/archives/fall-2011/kaplan-darvil/.
7. For a discussion of new legal industry business models see Williams, J.,

C., Platt, A., & Lee, J., *Disruptive Innovation: New Models of Legal Practice*, WorkLifeLaw, UC Hastings College of the Law (2015). See: http://worklifelaw.org/wp-content/uploads/2015/09/Disruptive-Innovations-New-Models-of-Legal-Practice-webNEW.pdf.

8. A yearly salary of $180,000 is fast becoming the Big Law standard for first-year associates. *See e.g.* Lee, S., *5 Potential Pitfalls Of The Associate Pay Hike Craze*, Law360 (Jul. 5, 2016). See: https://www.law360.com/articles/813536/5-potential-pitfalls-of-the-associate-pay-hike-craze.
9. See id.
10. See Germaine, *supra* note 3.
11. Beck, S., *The Wachtell Way of E-Discovery*, The American Lawyer (Feb. 1, 2016), http://www.americanlawyer.com/id=1202747505858/The-Wachtell-Way-of-EDiscovery-?mcode=0&curindex=0&curpage=ALL; *see also* Eric Kroh, *Robots The Latest Threat To Associates And The Billable Hour*, Law360 In-Depth (Jul. 16, 2016), http://www.law360.com/in-depth/articles/816737.
12. Germaine, *supra* note 3; Aebra Coe, *What Will Happen To Law Firms If Another Recession Hits?*, Law360 (Jun. 6, 2016). See: http://www.law360.com/articles/803483/what-will-happen-to-law-firms-if-another-recession-hits-.; see also Cohen, M., A., *Corporate Counsel: Consumer Becomes Provider*, Law360 (May 12, 2016), https://www.law360.com/articles/793919.

Chapter 5: Developing a CI function in a resource-constrained environment

By Annie Youngblood, manager of business intelligence at Pillsbury Winthrop Shaw Pittman

It is no surprise that law firms are operating in an increasingly cost-sensitive environment, where buzz-words such as "value-add" and "alternative fees" have become part of the everyday vernacular. It is a universe of dichotomy; clients want to save money and lawyers want to make money.

In a 2014 report from Altman Weil, a majority of law firms surveyed agreed that factors such as price competition, commoditization of legal work, and the onslaught of non-traditional service providers were permanent fixtures on the new "legal landscape"[1]. In addition to stagnant demand and pricing pressures, that means the legal industry is watching savvy new providers snap up work.

It is challenging to operate as support staff in such an environment. But winning the hearts (and wallets) of managing partners and chiefs and senior directors is largely about changing the way we think. Competitive intelligence is not a line item. It is not a budget allocation. It is value service that drives revenue and gives you a leg-up on the myriad law firms and attorneys that know very little about what their clients actually do.

It's a mentality that can be applied whether you're looking to add to a growing roster of CI analysts and professionals or simply looking to get your department off the ground.

Gaining buy-in

The first component of supporting that money-making mentality is making the case for demand. This is where preparation and data come into play. Just as an attorneys would prep to pitch major Fortune 500 companies, so it should be on the journey seeking additional resources.

The first – and most difficult step – is using data to establish need. Whether there's already a formal request process for business research and analysis, or the firm is looking to put one in place, be sure to collect as much data as is feasible. Borrowing a page out of journalism's textbooks, gaining buy-in should start with at least three months of data regarding the who, what, when, and how much of information requests. If there is not yet a central repository for such information, consider tapping the firm's information services team, business developers, and even financial analysts to get a sense of which attorneys are requesting what information and from whom.

This is not a statistics or economics equation; the goal is in fact to illustrate need across multiple departments and attorneys. Are there certain practice sections that require information more than others? Are there individual high-billing attorneys looking for support across major pitches? What is total demand? And, if possible, how much staff time (i.e. non-billable) is spent on doing such work?

The advantage of collecting data is twofold; it quantifies need and can help determine attorney and staff champions. Those champions will be helping support the need for additional resources and each of them has different skin in the game. Take the time to understand that bias. In most instances, the prized possession of such individuals is time. Will an additional resource allow a firm librarian to spend more time on billable requests? Will a new CI function allow a business developer to refocus efforts on creating a new focus team? Can a new CI analyst make room for associates to concentrate on client matters as opposed to company research?

Process, process, process

The manufacturing concept of Lean Six Sigma relies on the collaboration of individuals to remove waste from within an organization – literally making it leaner. It is a concept that is now being progressively applied across industries such as healthcare and law and can be applied on a micro level to growing or building a competitive intelligence function.

Process improvement means taking the data dump out of information dissemination. Again, this aligns with the time imperative. Instead of sending 150 pages of SEC filings to an attorney to decipher, pulling out key pieces of information saves time and money and could offer nuggets that might previously have been overlooked.

In other words, take the demand you've spent so long establishing and map out a process for satisfying that need. Here, the CI professional takes data and makes it actionable, providing a centralized resource for information.

"Centralized" is the key word. Law firms, especially larger ones, tend to suffer from major information silos across multiple practices and time zones. In the pitch for additional resources, the process component is the need for structure with an additional benefit. Through centralizing the request process, the CI professional becomes the nerve center of research and analysis – tapping additional resources when necessary and connecting professionals and attorneys when prudent.

Take this made-up but realistic example. A California partner requests monitoring on desalination activities along the coast. Separately, a partner in New York seeks information on private equity investors in the water space. If both partners use the same process to request such information, the firm is in position to consider a more holistic, end-to-end offering.

People

There really is no substitute for hard work. Finding, training, and growing CI professionals, particularly at the onset of a new department, can make or break your firm's efforts in this space. All the data and processes in the world won't make up for employees who lack initiative, drive, or creativity. In a resource-constrained environment, this fact becomes amplified.

When hiring external candidates to grow or develop this role, consider those from outside the legal profession with research and analytical skills. An affinity group of CI professionals from a dozen US law firms outlined the traits they felt were most important in hiring new CI professionals. Intellectual curiosity, perseverance, resourcefulness, and team spirit were at the top of the list.

There is, however, one way to avoid the pitfalls (personality and money alike) that come with recruiting external candidates: look within. In many law firms, CI responsibilities are already split among a slew of colleagues. By formalizing their involvement and providing training, you've eliminated a potentially detrimental unknown. At one Am Law 100 firm, the CI department is supplemented with staff from the library and client services teams. The "CI focus group" received extensive training on developing insightful company and industry dossiers for dissemination to partners. These colleagues provide support on about half of requests when bandwidth allows. The outcome is win-win: the staff member learns new skills and their departments receive positive firmwide recognition for their role in supporting a new, revenue generating service. By recruiting a handful of these types of personalities (many of whom are seeking professional development opportunities), it is possible to formalize and grow the CI function using existing resources from across the firm.

Take initiative

Your CI department will not create or grow itself. Being unseen and unheard is not uncommon in law firms, particularly in situations where support staff operate from a shared services environment. Building and growing this function requires a bit of pizazz and a willingness to approach various senior leaders with new ideas. We all know law firms aren't exactly hubs of innovation. It's common to hear a lot of "no", "not right now", or the most common "this is how we've always done it". Learning to craft your pitch with data, processes, systems, and people is key, but it's still possible you'll be told "no".

This is where those champions come back into play. Pick your horse. Taking the initiative to build and grow the firm's CI function means approaching certain partners or senior staff and offering a product or service they've not yet seen. In these cases, that product should be polished and refined. Are there target companies on which an attorney or practice group is focused? Is there a particularly adept senior associate that might be interested in formulating plans for the firm to take on legal issues in a bourgeoning area of law? Reading business plans and having conversations with business developers and attorneys can help guide this type of initiative.

Start small. Create a refined newsletter, provide an insightful dossier on a company, ask questions, and solicit feedback. For example, a handful of CI professionals throughout the Am Law 100 provide company briefs as a first step in growing their department. These are one-page documents that provide high-level information on a company (overview, news, outside counsel) prior to a meeting. It is not rocket science. There is no analysis. But lawyers love these documents because they can quickly scan them and gain a better understanding of what is important to a client or prospect. There is no data dump. By knowing what companies or topics are of interest to certain groups of people, the CI professional can offer that "low-hanging" fruit as a helpful introduction to this new service – and it doesn't cost a thing.

Solicit and implement feedback

A little history. Partnerships of more than three lawyers were fairly rare before the Civil War. Commercial pressures forced growth and, by 1898, 25 firms had five lawyers and another 32 had more than five. By 1915, there were 104 firms with five lawyers, and 136 with more than five. "Full service" commercial firms began to appear in centers like New York – firms like the Blatchford (that became Cravath, Swaine & Moore) and Shearman & Sterling. During this time, law firms created a new category of lawyers – associates.

Fast forward to 2016 and things look awfully similar. In fact, the legal industry has continued to grow its business model under the same structure it utilized more than 100 years ago. And so it shouldn't come as a surprise that there will be at least a few colleagues that will work to derail plans or put the kibosh on new ideas.

Make these people part of the process. Solicit their ideas and feedback (which could be negative) and do something with it. Most of the time, these types of colleagues need to feel like they are part of the process, that they came up with a helpful idea – in no uncertain terms, they want to feel useful. That is not to say they will be your greatest cheerleaders. Getting these colleagues to neutral is a more realistic expectation. How would they present information? What publications do they read? What are their thoughts on an emerging industry or legal issue? Once you've collected this feedback, show tangible activity. Implement these ideas to the extent possible. Maybe it's a short newsletter product, or making a minor change to an existing process. You might find that these ideas are among the best and most realistic you'll receive in the course of building the department.

Track outcomes

Show them the money. There is no greater purpose here. And let's be clear about something: competitive intelligence is by no means the sole driver of revenue. There are a million factors that go into winning and expanding work. But consider this: if understanding a client's business makes up a mere five percent of the factors that combine to win new work, one large engagement – or a handful of smaller matters – is likely to pay for your department. This is where that money-making mentality finally shows its colors.

In order for this to become a reality within your CI department, every project, every request, and every small piece of information that goes out the door must be tracked. Say goodbye to the black hole of information. Bid farewell to documents for which you never received feedback. At this stage, your CI department should have a process in place by which data is easily collected. Tracking outcomes is easier if you know the attorneys who are requesting information, the name of the client or target, and whether the data is being used for a pitch or an informal lunch meeting.

There are countless sources of this type of information that your firm might or might not make available. New matter reports, pitch activity reports, and the firm's financial database are just a few options for determining outcomes. The best source of this information, however, always will be people. Relationships with business developers and attorneys can play a key role in tracking outcomes. Consider sending quarterly emails to business developers about the project on which you supported with the goal of reminding them about past and ongoing efforts. Many will likely be thankful for a nudge that they need to check back with an attorney on a focus initiative or target. Ask an attorney how a lunch or pitch meeting went and offer to provide ongoing monitoring on the topic or prospect.

The other benefit to tracking outcomes is measuring time spent and workload. For those departments looking to add staff, this is a key component. How many requests were fielded and by how many people? Law firm CI departments easily field hundreds of these types of requests a year. How is that time spent? On important, analytical revenue-driving efforts? On company briefs for last minute lunch meetings? Which attorneys are requesting information? Often, having high billers as frequent customers can be the only ammunition needed to add staff or purchase new tools.

Ready to launch

Resources will continue to be strained across the legal industry for the foreseeable future. It's a situation that calls for the greatest understanding of a client's needs in many years. Knowing what to offer, when to offer it, and to whom to pitch are an absolute necessity. Just ask Japan's Bridgestone Corp. A lawyer for the company's American unit, speaking at a legal marketing event, told a compelling story about the impact of the Ebola outbreak on the organization. *The Wall Street Journal* – and tons of other media outlets – chronicled how managers huddled around a rubber-tree and googled "Ebola" when the first case arrived at the company's Liberian unit. What followed was a crash course in calming a massive epidemic.

Amid the slew of law firms and attorneys working with Bridgestone, a single attorney from a single law firm reached out to the Bridgestone attorney speaking at this event to commend the company's work in Africa. Now, that attorney and that law firm are top of mind. It's a simple story about the power of small acts.

Competitive intelligence can unearth and nurture such relationships, whether as a formal function or as a more ad-hoc, though centralized, process. The components to developing such a service are plentiful and varied, though perhaps none is more important than persistence.

Developing and growing your firm's CI function might call for a fair bit of trial and error – but as the industry is beginning to understand the importance of change, you just might find a more willing audience than you anticipate.

Reference

1. Altman Weil, "Law Firms in Transition", 2014. See: http://www.altmanweil.com/dir_docs/resource/f68236ab-d51f-4d81-8172-96e8d47387e3_document.pdf

Chapter 6: Proactively delivering information services

By Marlene Gebauer, director of knowledge solutions at Greenberg Traurig

Legal information professionals have historically been the go-to resource for busy legal practitioners in need of a variety of different content and resources. The call-and-response research request model for legal, competitive, or business intelligence has been standard for many years. An attorney makes a request and a researcher/librarian provides a response or resource (and perhaps asks some questions along the way for clarification). This system still works, but in the age of project management, workflows and automation, it can be improved, which benefits clients, attorneys and information professionals.

Challenges of the traditional model:

- Misunderstanding the request; and
- Rushed timeframe to answer the request

Requests can be misinterpreted, sometimes because of the communication method, lack of requester clarity, or lack of comprehension on the part of the information professional. Time spent on clarifying or revising a response, while necessary, is still additional time and money spent. Similarly, when requests arrive on tight deadlines, responses may be incomplete or erroneous because there is not sufficient time to fully vet and answer requests.

Improving the process

There is a way to improve quality control in the request workflow and make it a more proactive process:

1. Map out matter milestones for delivery
2. Identify common types of requests based on each milestone
3. Create delivery templates
4. Automate all processes as much as possible
5. Establish a feedback loop to ensure the process and deliverables are useful and timely

While there are examples on the internet that can serve as a base, for future acceptance of a new model, it is important to map matters in accord with how the legal practitioners in your firm view them. Inviting an attorney, hopefully one endorsed by the impacted practice groups, along with a person familiar with matter mapping, to be part of the initial process, will help ensure your organization's view of matter milestones is not only positive but will also encourage later adoption of the entire process by other legal practitioners.[1]

Matter mapping

Matter mapping does not have to incorporate all types of matters. You may wish to focus on practices that have the most impact on your department initially and expand into others later. You may also find that certain practice areas may share milestones, partially or exactly, and these milestones can therefore be used for different groups somewhat interchangeably.

Once the overarching map is made, the marrying of information services to each milestone begins. There is no exact science to this analysis. Services like business and competitive intelligence, legal research, licensing of online information services, and book orders can occur at different times, multiple times, and at the same time in the life of a matter. Application of evidence-based analysis, combined with requester feedback and the experience of information professionals[2] provides a good roadmap. Your information center's statistics on research requests, acquisitions records (print and digital) and use of tools such as online research platforms, eBooks, and print are critical to the analysis.

Using a litigation example, in the client acquisition phase, a review of research request statistics may show that attorneys commonly request an industry analysis, company/competitor profiles, news, a litigation analysis for the potential client, and legal competitor experience. They may also request internal firm experience information, litigation analysis, and financial data for work similar to the RFP or pitch. These can be noted as materials to compose and disseminate as part of a package. Most of these same materials can be used at the case assessment phase of litigation to plan strategy and manage client expectations and can be noted for that milestone. Once the analysis is completed, attorney feedback can help fine-tune the final deliverable.

A different example involves onboarding of lateral attorneys. Based on their prior firm experience, laterals often arrive with certain expectations of what information resources will be available to them. There may be an inability to replicate the exact information platform desired for a variety of reasons. When this is the case, analysis of the metrics from online catalogs, ordering records from others in the relevant practice and evaluations of information tools[3] can be used, with the blessing of the practice groups, to determine basic access to resources for onboarded attorneys. The platform may vary from practice to practice, based on the analysis, and a method for request escalation and adjustment will need to be in place, but initial delivery is normalized and proactive upon onboarding, saving time and effort. In both this example and the earlier research example, the deliverables can be distilled and bundled into a templated package.

Delivery templates

Templates are a key component to the proactive and automated delivery of information services. They ensure, to the best extent possible, that attorneys are getting consistent, normalized, base-level deliverables. Without the template and associated completion process, there will be inconsistency involving use of resources, selection of content and presentation. This is human nature. Every information professional will address a project with a different perspective, based on their past experiences and influences. This can impact the final product.

While a certain degree of flexibility is built into a request-driven model based on its customized nature, in a proactive model success is built on a common understanding of the final product. The deliverable has to be consistent in content, references, and presentation. If the end products vary significantly, the expectation and trust of the requester is compromised and the system fails.

It is important to note that using templates to assist in standardized delivery does not take away from customized, curated delivery but can enhance and increase the demand for that work if it is highlighted appropriately. Think of templates as the appetizer to a meal: small bites which may or may not suffice an appetite. If a requestor desires more, you have an entire menu to choose from for a more substantial entrée. Templates provide the base information everyone will need at a particular matter milestone. Templates can and should be coupled with a checklist of additional available customized service. The items on this list have already been mapped out as relevant to the milestone so can easily be added, along with a brief explanation if needed.

For example, as part of the case assessment analysis, all practitioners need a judicial assessment.[4] Let us assume, that requesters ask for a judge's education, experience as a judge and practitioner, familiarity with types of actions, motion/ruling practice, time to resolve a case and associations with firms, parties, and counsel. This information can be sourced and compiled into a standard template and delivered with a checklist of other research options such as causes of action, judicial influences, statute of limitations, filing and news alerts, and regulatory research. Requesters check off what they want, add other desired items and then the research can be performed.

Templates are not necessarily easy to get right and there is a lot of work behind the scenes to create them. Even knowing what should be included in the deliverables, before you can craft a template, you need to identify the tools that will provide the information. This will aid in creating an optimal workflow and training program for the information professionals, so they consistently use the same tools and format, preferably with the department's branding. Other considerations include storing, upkeep and access/searchability of templated deliverables and ROI on time, money and resources spent in development, implementation, and regular execution.

Automating the delivery of information services

The proactivity and automation of delivery of information services depends a great deal on some method of notification and a process to follow once that notification is received. Notification is not a request for information; instead it is an event that triggers an action process. In some instances, such as requests for RFPs, it is more difficult to predict what information will be required for a response, so a proactive package deliverable may not be appropriate. However, if appropriate notification for a pitch is provided, the base level package can be created with custom deliverables as needed.

Automated notification, within a complex organization can be challenging. While we all receive notifications through email and text,[5] there is a challenge in day-to-day work to identify points when and why notification should be made, how, and to whom. Matter mapping assists in identifying the when and why, but doesn't address the how and to whom questions. To address those questions, we need to look at existing notification systems and evaluate how they can be better incorporated into the automated information process, as well as innovative tools that may be able to take an organization to a higher level of automation.

Existing tools can be repurposed, and this may be preferable to quickly implement a new process at a minimal expense. One notification system that can be utilized is a robust docket monitoring platform. Clerks and paralegals already rely heavily on these systems for case management. Setting appropriate alerts to be delivered to an information team can trigger templated work such as assessments on judges, opposing counsel, parties, and jurisdictions. New attorney alerts provide another opportunity to deliver proactively. The information team may already receive new attorney alerts as part of the resource access and password management process. Some changes to internal workflow will allow them to provide an onboarding information roadmap and training schedule to new hires. Similarly, new matter alerts can also be used to initiate the creation of industry and company intelligence, filing alerts, and legal news alerts for both attorneys and clients.

These are all adequate solutions, but they all require a certain degree of human interaction to initiate the process. Humans must create a search and set up alerts, and while this may seem like a small thing, trying to implement this across hundreds if not thousands of data points can take a considerable amount of staff time. It is detailed, repetitive work and not everyone enjoys it. There may not be adequate staff to handle the work. Based on the need to manage other more valuable department duties, the cost associated with devoting staff to this work may not make sense. Thus, we look to tools that can help automate the process.

As far as more advanced tools go, there are workflow platforms that can be used if your firm is willing to invest in them. Developing tools in-house is another option, which requires adequate staffing, and skill sets to build, maintain, and update. Expert systems[6] and "bots"[7] can also be considered to automate notification and delivery. Expert systems work like a make-your-own-adventure – based on selections you make, certain things happen. The systems are programmed in the background to ensure certain tasks are initiated based on choices made and to keep a record of this. Bots are also rules-based tools and can map and perform basic business process and actions, such as repetitive data entry.[8]

Blockchain technology[9] is another potential solution. It already has applications in payment, lending, and digital currency. It can be used to create a step-by-step, agreed-upon and distributed protocol that is time-stamped, is able to be linked to individuals, can be tracked in real time as each block (task) is validated and is easy to verify. For example, when a new matter report is generated an automatic notification can be sent to identified parties that a task (block) is pending for them to complete. Upon completion, the blockchain (ledger of tasks) is updated and a notification can automatically be sent to advise others of the next set of tasks.

Use of any of these innovative tools would make process automation and proactive delivery of services easier for any information center. Perhaps more importantly, it would make it easier to combine process and deliverables from across an entire organization. Portals, practice pages, and communal workspaces serve this purpose today but they are partial and static solutions. There is still a great deal of human work in the background to keep these tools updated, functioning, and current. Automation plays a minimal role.

To get a sense of how a more automated system would work, let's look at a couple of examples first applying an expert, and then a blockchain model. In applying an expert system to the delivery of an onboarding package, members of all relevant departments[10] would have access. An if-then decision tree of questions would be answered. There would be one decision tree for everyone, but based on how users answer the questions, they would be directed on different paths associated with their tasks. The paths could provide instruction on tasks to complete or could assist in completion of the task itself.[11] This can be used, for example, to execute on security protocols or draft a welcome package.

In applying blockchain to case assessment/pretrial preparation deliverables, members of all relevant groups would have access to and be assigned to blocks (tasks). Once a matter cleared conflicts,[12] notification could automatically be sent to the user assigned to the designated blocks. This can be used, for example, to execute on building a jurisdictional profile or litigation experience assessment.[13] Once done and verified, the next set of relevant users are notified that there are blocks (tasks) waiting with their own unique set of instructions.[14] The process continues until completion.

Establishing a feedback loop

Circling back to our components list, the last step in the proactive delivery model is establishing a feedback loop to ensure the process and deliverables are useful and timely. The importance of this last component cannot be over emphasized. Feedback is critical to ensure that the attorneys find value in the process and deliverable. If they do not, there is no business purpose, no ROI, and consequently no reason to continue.

If the attorneys do find value, they may have suggestions for additional content, alternate delivery methods, or a completely new deliverable. The evaluation does not end when adjustments are made; it is just the beginning. It is indeed a loop; the process is ongoing in order to stay in line with the business needs of the attorneys and the organization.

Getting feedback from busy practitioners is always a challenge, but it can be accomplished. Every organization will have a different method, so it is important to understand what will work in your business culture. Having an evangelist or establishing liaisons to relevant practices who support process change can go a long way in getting attorneys' attention. Do not be afraid to use the influence of others to get your message across. It is a collaborative way to make your initiative successful.

Other methods of gathering feedback include surveys, meetings (telephone, video, and in-person), presentations (in-person, video, and recorded), contests, and games. In using any of these, it is key that the message be succinct and engaging and the information sought be critical to your purpose. It is also important to help practitioners understand the business purpose of the initiative and how their engagement benefits their practice. This better positions the information center as a thought leader in the delivery of legal services.

Our changing legal landscape requires innovative approaches which highlight the valuable services information professionals provide. The need for efficiency coupled with cost concerns requires information centers to streamline and automate work. Application of a process and identification of key milestones which deliver basic information are also necessary to increase quality control and manage expectation of our organizations, while still providing custom, crafted deliverables. Adjusting traditional models of information service, mapping matters, repurposing existing tools, and processes and investing in new ones are all areas where information professionals can lead the discussion and implementation in their organizations, further enhancing their reputation as visionaries in the knowledge and information arena.

References

1. While we are discussing information services in this chapters, having a high-level matter map can be a jumping off point for a variety of support service processes.
2. If you have research attorneys on your information team who have practiced law, they can offer insights regarding at what point specific services should be delivered. Similarly, all experienced information professionals should have a sense of basic milestones and what is needed at each based on work performed over time.

3. The information center is regularly evaluating and re-evaluating information tools on the market. Having a template and a schedule in place to evaluate competitor products is useful to determine if the overall information platform is sufficient or has gaps and to educate new arrivals of preferred products when their familiar resources cannot be purchased.
4. This is true whether or not the practitioner has experience with a judge. Practitioners simply may not be aware of certain facts. Sometimes, subjective knowledge differs from evidence-based findings. The marrying of both provides the best picture. Also, an assessment can change over time as a judge's experience changes, so should be revisited periodically.
5. Amber Alerts and automated office closings are examples.
6. "An expert system is a computer system that emulates the decision-making ability of a human expert. Expert systems are designed to solve complex problems by reasoning about knowledge, represented mainly as if–then rules rather than through conventional procedural code." Wikipedia contributors. "Expert system." *Wikipedia, The Free Encyclopedia.* Wikipedia, The Free Encyclopedia, May 2017
7. A bot is a device or piece of software that can execute commands, reply to messages, or perform routine tasks, as online searches, either automatically or with minimal human intervention (often used in combination). *Dictionary.com* Random House, 2004, July 2017
8. King, "AT&T Employees Automate Repetitive Tasks with Software Bots", *Wall Street Journal,* 15 May 2016
9. "Block chain is a distributed database that is used to maintain a continuously growing list of records, called *blocks.* Each block contains a timestamp and a link to a previous block. A blockchain is typically managed by a peer-to-peer network collectively adhering to a protocol for validating new blocks. By design, blockchains are inherently resistant to modification of the data." Wikipedia contributors. "Blockchain." *Wikipedia, The Free Encyclopedia.* Wikipedia, The Free Encyclopedia, Jul. 2017
10. For example, technology, information services, professional development, and litigation support
11. Drafting language for communication or documents based on distinctions in practice groups is one example of how expert systems can aid in task completion.
12. This is a perfect-world example. Any designated point could trigger the chain.
13. The system can also auto-execute some actions – such as sending auto-generated emails to multiple parties.
14. If part of the chain breaks down – if someone fails to complete the tasks assigned or delays in completing their task – there is clear accountability. There is a person associated with the block along with associated timestamps – this cannot be altered without corruption of the chain becoming obvious.

Chapter 7:

Moving from content aggregation to content intelligence

By Steven A. Lastres, director of knowledge management services at Debevoise and Plimpton LLP

In order to give clients their best advice, law firms need to ensure that their lawyers are informed about the latest news, legal developments, decisions, and deals – as well as keeping an eye on the competition. Forward-thinking firms are taking content aggregation tools used for over a decade to the next level by providing content intelligence platforms.

Content intelligence combines business intelligence with content management. This helps law firms manage a vast amount of unstructured data and helps the lawyer make smart strategic and tactical decisions. The primary benefit of content intelligence is that it delivers personalized information to each individual or team within an organization based on their particular focus and personal preferences. Some of the user features include real-time current awareness dashboards with the ability for lawyers to search across the entire data warehouse of the firm's premium subscription services and internet resources and providing them with the ability to create their own alerts. Additionally, by taking advantage of the technology and the expertise of information professionals embedded within practice groups, client teams, industry sectors, and market teams, firms can publish curated e-newsletters that pinpoint the specific needs of their audience more accurately.

Actionable intelligence is also being pushed directly onto practice groups, client teams, and industry intranet pages as well as their lawyers' mobile devices for easy access. Lawyers can now keep up on a real-time basis with the latest relevant information that affects their practice and clients, making them not only knowledgeable but proactive in servicing their clients.

The need to move beyond content aggregation

The use of content aggregation tools in law firms is nothing new. Most firms adopted these tools almost a decade ago as a way to solve information overload. In the past, lawyers were inundated with dozens of daily emails from vendors pushing their publications directly to a lawyer's email inbox and clogging the communication channel meant primarily for clients. Content aggregation tools solved this problem – one email a day contained all the updates, and so became widely adopted in law firms. As good as they were, content aggregation tools are no longer an effective solution for delivering current awareness. What changed? With the age of the internet came the disaggregation of the major legal publishers. A handful of legal and business publishers mushroomed into thousands of publishers from traditional media as well as social media. As a result, there has been exponential growth in the sheer volume of current awareness content that we are pushing to our end-users. Furthermore, the business downturn in the legal industry since 2008 increased lawyer's focus on business development – reducing the time lawyers have to spend keeping up with current awareness both for the practice and business of law.

Due to the convergence of exponential growth in content sources and the breadth of what lawyers need to know to be successful as practitioners and business leaders, lawyers have shifted how they consume current awareness. It is no longer customary for a lawyer to read an electronic newsletter cover to cover. Instead, lawyers scan the headlines of current awareness content search for specific content on a real-time basis. Many traditional aggregation tools have not kept up with the changing needs of users. This has led to a demand for a smarter tool that can help lawyers effectively search and filter for the most relevant and actionable information related to the reader's specific preferences based on their practice, clients, deals, etc.

The role of information professionals in delivering content intelligence

In law firms, there is an expectation that information professionals should understand what specific content is required for the groups they support, but also the custom individual practitioners need to be successful. It is no longer acceptable to simply push RSS or XML feeds that publishers provide to us as they update their own publications on a 24-hour cycle. In fact, our users are looking for tools that provide not only content itself, but also for ways to put that content within context, minus the noise, so they can focus on what is important to them. As stewards of the firm's information resources, how do information professionals advance from simply providing content aggregation to providing content intelligence?

Checklist of functionality to consider in a content intelligence platform

Taxonomy and search

The backbone of any content intelligence system is the taxonomy that enables information professionals to accurately and automatically categorize content by facets such as subject, client, industry, geography, practice group, etc. Look for relevant, pre-built search taxonomies to aid in reducing irrelevant content. Overlay your firm's custom-built taxonomy with the platform's out-of-the-box taxonomy. Remember that a robust taxonomy leads to more effective and efficient searching of resources and on-point content delivery. It is highly recommended that in evaluating any content intelligence platform you spend a significant amount of time testing to ensure you receive expected results.

Look to see what the underlying search engine is that the vendor is using. Is it a proprietary search engine or is it an industry leader like IBM Watson? The more robust the search engine, the better results you will be able to deliver to your end users and the easier for end users to find content on their own through the platform. Does the search engine provide you with robust filtering capabilities to narrow and sort search results?

Source management

The old adage of "garbage in, garbage out" applies to content systems as well as databases. It is critical to your success to evaluate the source management tool which enables information professionals to manage all of the organization's content sources (free, premium, and firm proprietary content) so they can pick the right set of information. Be aware that some vendors may charge you to add premium content. Do not overlook the ability to connect to your firm's automated HR system or Active Directory data so that you can programmatically assign sources to certain individuals, teams, and/or firm-wide. Does the platform provide the ability to control the relevancy of sources by pushing articles from certain sources higher up in search results or by excluding certain sources?

Reporting is a critical feature of any source management tool and the ability to obtain detailed metrics by content title, user, and distribution list. Having granular metrics about content title, users, and distribution equips the information professional with objective data about usage. This is invaluable when the time comes to negotiate licensing agreements that are aligned with "actual" usage and to see unambiguously what content your users find valuable.

Content delivery

The platform must have the ability to seamlessly integrate content in any standard format: RSS, XML, PDF, URL links, e-mails, Twitter feeds, and website scraping into one platform. Integration helps your users on any of the firm's platform that they choose to use, including the intranet, extranet and mobile apps with focused content and important information relating to specific practices, industries, and clients. Be mindful that your use of these formats should conform to the license agreements you negotiate with your premium content vendors. There is a growing trend among marketing professionals to use content intelligence platforms to distribute internal firm newsletters within the content aggregation tool as well as ingesting external client advice memos from other firms to monitor competitors. Therefore, keep in mind that there are many different types of content formats beyond RSS or XML formats that the platform needs to accommodate.

Curation and publishing

As lawyers continue to get buried in an avalanche of content, curated newsletters are now a critical tool for information professionals to get the attention of an information saturated audience. Curated newsletters should be created not only for specific practice areas, but also for market teams, management, and industry groups. As more informational professionals are embedded into various legal and marketing teams, they become keenly aware of what content those groups need. That insight helps the newsletter editors to cherry-pick content of greatest relevance from all of the content sets that the group receives. A well curated newsletter is extremely valuable: it saves the lawyers from having to scroll through and navigate all the content that a typical content aggregation tool pushes to them. And anything that saves lawyers time is golden! What we now hear from our lawyers, is that "if I don't have time to read Law360, the BNA newsletter, the Wolters Kluwer newsletter, and the other alerts that I receive each day, I just read the curated newsletter because I am guaranteed to not miss any critical content that's relevant to my practice." In fact, it is now commonplace for partners to regularly interact with the information professionals to tweak curated newsletters to focus on new areas of interest or potential clients. This level of collaboration previously was uncommon aside from the occasional research request.

For information professionals, this has opened up a new avenue of collaboration with firm leadership, partners, and other decision makers at the firm and has raised their profile as valued partners in supporting the business and practice of law.

Competitive intelligence and data analytics

With the influx of big data in the legal industry, it is critically important that your content intelligence platform automate the gathering of competitive information, business news, and social media using an analytics engine designed to find, analyze, display, and disseminate intelligence to help drive results within your organization. When lawyers receive daily alerts via email there is a lack of insight and context into the portfolio of feeds that they are receiving. Data analytics can illuminate this large array of content. Cloud tags by industry, entity, persons named, and geography can help make sense of multiple news stories. Bar charts show what's trending on a particular day for a particular client or particular feed. These tools give readers insight that cannot be replicated by traditional daily email pushes.

In terms of media content, it is important today more than ever that we include social media channels in addition to traditional media. There are a number of providers that are scraping content from social media which has become important for law firms in sending out client advice memos, press releases, and other information onto social media platforms such as LinkedIn. Social media has become another important channel for marketing and business development initiatives.

Dashboard view of my alerts

Lawyers are not stock traders. They don't sit in front of a Bloomberg terminal waiting with bated breath for market data and news to complete a trade. But lawyers do need to be kept abreast on a real-time basis of significant legislative, regulatory, and deal information that impacts their clients and practice. As a result, a once-a-day email push, perhaps an afternoon update is no longer sufficient. Lawyers want to know about breaking news so they can be the first to inform their client. However, by sending out real-time alerts to a lawyer's inbox we run the risk of bombarding their inbox with a plethora of new additional emails and so we defeat the purpose of what content aggregation tools were meant to solve. Instead, by providing the user with a dashboard view of their alerts on their desktop or mobile device, they are able to easily view and consume breaking alerts on all of their current awareness alerts as well as disseminate the information to clients and internal team members, subject to copyright permission.

Real-time alerts

Confirm that your content aggregation tool has the ability to push real-time alerts within their tool onto a user's dashboard or practice group or client team page as opposed to clogging up a lawyer's email inbox. Arguably, while there may be times where a specific alert needs to be pushed by email, what is needed is the flexibility to offer it in both the content aggregation tool as well as in email.

End user creation and management of custom alerts

While many partners do not fully utilize many of the technology tools deployed at law firms, millennial lawyers are a more appreciative audience. A content intelligence platform should provide the end user who wants to create his or her own custom alerts with the tools to do so. Those self-help users ought to be able to edit and delete alerts directly from the user interface. Those user created alerts may not substitute for the sophisticated alerts created by information professionals, however they do provide the end user with options for keeping themselves informed.

The market players in the legal sector and how to evaluate their tools

There are some excellent content intelligence tools in the legal market. Below, I mention those that as of the writing of this article are the serious market players in the legal sector. Remember, what makes a great tool for one law firm may make it a poor choice at another firm. It is incumbent upon every information professional to perform their due diligence review. Survey your lawyers and conduct focus groups to determine their needs before you start shopping. Create a detailed request for proposal (RFP) focusing on the content, features, and functionality you need delivered to solve the business problems you are trying to solve for your users. Since no tool is likely to check off all the boxes in your RFP, you may want to include a contract provision to engage the vendor to develop the functionality you need within a short period after signing an agreement. Pay special attention to the service-level agreement to ensure your vendor can deliver on a platform that works as close to 24/7 as possible with minimal downtime for maintenance and upgrades.

While you can use your RFP checklist to narrow down your choices to a few tools, in order to understand which tool really gets you closest to solving your firm's content needs, you must conduct at least two pilots to kick the tires. The pilot will provide you with valuable feedback to understand what the tool does well and what you thought it could do, but it really doesn't do. Pilots should include information professionals and end users comprised of lawyers and marketing professionals. Good candidates to evaluate a new tool are the top complainers at your firm who constantly say they're drowning in information. Don't be side-tracked into looking at products that only have a great administrative tool that help the information professionals better manage content but that do not address the needs of your users. Focus first on what it is that the lawyers need because they are the core audience that will be using the tool. Next, look for a tool that has a simple and easy-to-use interface. Unnecessary complexity will prove to be a barrier to adoption. Secondarily, focus on the needs of the information professionals.

Assuming you find a tool that has all of the bells and whistles that you could possibly want, provide a list of all of the publishers and titles you would like to disseminate to your users. Confirm that the content intelligence tool vendor has executed licenses and distribution agreements with those publishers to ingest and distribute the content that you want to send to your lawyers. This is particularly important with your premium content sources. Neutral content intelligence tools that do not create and sell their own content like InfoNGen, Manzama, Ozmosys, and Vable are likely to benefit from close relationships with all legal and business publishers than content intelligence tools that also publish and sell content like Bloomberg/BNA and Lexis. Be aware that some legal publishers like Lexis and Westlaw will require an additional agreement to allow their law firm clients to stream their content through a content intelligence tool.

Don't underestimate the deployment time that it takes to implement a content intelligence tool. It is highly suggested you use a project manager since it is likely to take a minimum of three months to get all of your feeds and alerts onto any new system as well as syncing users from your HR or AD system. Further, you will likely need to dedicate one or more full time equivalents (FTEs) to managing and maintaining the content intelligence platform. And do not overlook the need for some lawyer training and feedback loop.

What lawyers want most out of a content intelligence tool is the ability to keep up on a real-time basis with the latest relevant information that impacts their practice and clients, making them not only knowledgeable but proactive in servicing their clients. The closer your content intelligence strategy is aligned to the business strategy of your organization, the more successful you will be in meeting the needs of your lawyers and firm. As actionable information leads to better client service, you will look like the hero for delivering content intelligence to your organization.

Below is a brief synopsis of each of the market players in the legal sector:

- **BNAConvergence** – the strength of BNAConvergence, now part of Bloomberg Law, is the proprietary BNA legal newsletter content and the vast collection of Bloomberg sources. BNAConvergence provides pre-built dashboards that can be filtered to ensure relevance, and also provides deeper search capability and trending analysis. A mobile version is also available for on-the-go access.
- **InfoNgen** – describes itself as a real-time discovery engine for business, finance, and information professionals that automatically monitors and extracts highly relevant information. While a relative newcomer in the legal sector, it provides a sophisticated user portal platform that aggregates and indexes all content and automatically tags it with InfoNgen's robust meta-data.
- **LexisNexis Newsdesk** – is a relatively new product offering that came about as a result of the LexisNexis acquisition of Moreover Technologies in 2015. The combination of LexisNexis premium content that includes the Wall Street Journal and thousands of other business, legal, and news sources combined with the Moreover Technologies current awareness and media monitoring tool makes it a formidable competitor in the content intelligence space.
- **Manzama** – has developed a strong client base with law firm marketing departments primarily for monitoring a wider range of news and social media sources focused on business development and competitive intelligence. They also provide professionally prepared premium intelligence reports created by their in-house industry analysts.
- **Ozmosys** – was one of the first content aggregation, search, alerting, and content delivery tools used by large enterprises to control information overload. Ozmosys consolidates high-value information from leading content providers and publishers and removes barriers found in typical distribution methods. Most recently, Ozmosys has developed a new platform called Open Alerts which provides a customizable end user dashboard.

- **Vable** – formerly known as Linex, Vable is a UK-based content intelligence tool that has made significant inroads in the US with law firm clients. Their content automation platform was completely overhauled in late 2016 and now uses IBM Watson search to power its taxonomy and search engine.

Chapter 8:
How artificial intelligence is transforming legal research

By Jennifer Mendez, senior manager of KM firm solutions at Ogletree Deakins

The role of the legal researcher has changed significantly over the last decade. While there will likely always be a need for research, there appears to be a decrease in "traditional" reference requests. This is because the work of legal researchers has expanded beyond locating case law and legislative histories; they are also assisting with business development, competitive intelligence, and trend analysis. With so much change and disruption, how will the expansion of AI affect an already shifting research landscape?

What is artificial intelligence?

Before we can discuss the impact artificial intelligence is having and will have on legal research platforms, it is important to define AI. While some would like you to believe that robots will replace lawyers and legal researchers, I believe AI in legal is about making attorneys and researchers more efficient. AI in the legal research market is about teaching computers to process information in the way the researcher would, specifically around the human competences of reasoning, communication, and decision-making. AI in legal is about emulating the key cognitive elements that make legal researchers and lawyers, experts in their respective fields.

While the latest press coverage would have readers believe this is a new trend, applications of AI such as machine learning (ML) and Natural Language Processing (NLP) have been around for years and are at the core of several legal research platforms.

For those in the legal research space, it is obvious that the resources have improved by leaps and bounds over the last decade. Improvements to user interfaces, search algorithms, and information retrieval have resulted in databases that are not just powerful but easy to use as well. Some would argue the "big two", Lexis and Westlaw, have always been at the forefront of legal research innovation, but there are some newcomers that are shaking things up. Let us look at how conducting research in Lexis and Westlaw has changed over the years due to innovations in technology and the introduction of artificial intelligence and how some startups are disturbing the legal research market.

Westlaw

As a reminder of how far legal research has come, let's review a brief history of Thomson Reuters Westlaw. Westlaw started in the 1970s as a dial-up service. The company later introduced a dedicated terminal known as WALT (short for West Automatic Law Terminal).[1] By the 90s, Westlaw had moved to the internet. It continued to add databases and to work on improvements to the platform.

In 2010, however, Westlaw seemingly proclaimed their dedication to the future of search when they released WestSearch, the company's proprietary search engine. WestSearch focused on improvements to how West platforms handle natural language processing, machine learning, and information retrieval.[2] It was a clear indication that Westlaw would be focusing on AI as a way of improving their platform. This focus on plain language searching is a significant departure from how researchers use Westlaw. For the most sophisticated users, the power of systems like Westlaw lies within the searcher's ability to construct searches using Boolean logic. Also in 2010, Westlaw introduced Westlaw Next. Westlaw Next transformed the way users interacted with Westlaw, because researchers no longer had to select a database to search but could search all of Westlaw's content with a single action.[3]

In April 2016, Westlaw debuted several new features developed using applications of artificial intelligence.[4] Westlaw did not label them as such in any of their promotional materials, but based on what the technology allows researchers to do, most would make the connection. Westlaw Answers was promoted as a way to get specific answers to common types of legal questions. Researchers no longer had to go through a lengthy list of results to determine the elements of fraud in Minnesota. Instead, Westlaw Answers offers you the answer to this and similar questions. The user has the option to select a question from a type-ahead display, and the answer will appear above the remaining search results. This was Westlaw's first attempt at providing an answer to a question rather than having the researcher deduce the answer from a lengthy list of results. While terms and connectors searching still remains an important feature, artificial intelligence technologies call for simplified searching: simply pose a question as you would to a person and have the system generate a response.

Research Recommendations was the second of the enhancements, and it leverages natural language processing and machine learning to identify patterns in your document interactions during your session. This means that it does not just look at your current search, but the entirety of your searches and document views during your session. It then makes recommendations for additional relevant documents and Key Numbers to ensure the researcher has a complete view and does not miss anything pertinent.

Finally, Folder Analysis takes on a similar approach as it relates to the content saved in a researcher's Westlaw folders. This enhancement analyzes the text of the items saved to the folders, identifies the issues, and suggests additional relevant cases. Additionally, the results are visualized so the researcher can see graphical display of the issues with links to the appropriate content.

With such transformational changes to Westlaw's approach to search, future forays into artificial intelligence are sure to alter the way lawyers and legal researchers work.

LexisNexis

In 1973, Mead Data Center introduced LEXIS, a computer-assisted legal research system limited to Ohio and New York codes and cases, the U.S.code, and some federal case law. By 1980, Lexis included case law for all 50 states and the NEXIS service provided access to news from major sources. In 1993, Lexis launched a new "natural language" search feature, FREESTYLE. Over the next several decades, Lexis continued to improve its platform and to expand its reach with a number of mergers, acquisitions, and strategic alliances.

In November 2015, Lexis announced its acquisition of Lex Machina. Lex Machina's Legal Analytics software mines public court documents using natural language processing to help predict how a judge will rule in a certain type of case. With the Lexis relationship in place, Lex Machina will now have access to a significantly more information and more resources to expand the depth and breadth of their product. According to the press release, "The acquisition of Lex Machina is part of the ongoing LexisNexis commitment to offer modern, next-generation legal research solutions that harness the power of Big Data through natural language processing and machine learning to help legal professionals work more efficiently, make more informed decisions and drive success for their clients, practice and business."[5] In February 2017, Lexis announced it was integrating Lex Machina into its flagship online legal information solution Lexis Advance. Doing so gives a larger audience access to data analytics that results in actionable information.

In June 2017, LexisNexis also announced the acquisition of Ravel Law.[6] Similarly to Lex Machina, Ravel Law focuses on data analytics and leverages machine learning and natural language processing technologies. The technology allows users to uncover valuable information in order to help develop the best arguments to put in front of a particular judge.

Shortly after the Ravel Law acquisition, Lexis launched its response to Westlaw Answers: Lexis Answers. This feature brings another layer of AI to the Lexis Advance legal research platform. With Lexis Answers, a researcher can ask a natural-language question and get back the single-best answer in the form of a Lexis Answer Card. Again, this is a significant departure from the terms and connectors searching that is so familiar to Lexis users. Additionally, users will now see charts and graphs visualizing results where they only used to see text.

Given Lexis' history, it would not come as a surprise to see additional mergers, acquisitions, or strategic alliances with companies in the artificial intelligence space.

The newcomers

Unlike Lexis and Westlaw, which have transformed their platforms over the years, several newcomers have burst onto the legal research scene with a single promise: AI will transform the way you work.

ROSS Intelligence (powered by IBM Watson)

By now, most of us have seen IBM's supercomputer Watson win at Jeopardy.[7] The technology behind Watson is being used in multiple fields: health, financial services, education, and legal. ROSS Intelligence made its debut in 2014 and is promoted as "the world's first artificially intelligent attorney."[8] Built on ROSS Intelligence's proprietary legal AI framework, Legal Cortex, along with IBM's Watson technology, ROSS uses natural language processing and machine learning to identify citations relevant to particular legal questions. Simply put, it is the Siri or Alexa of legal research tools. Ask ROSS a question, and it will provide an answer. Additionally, the system is intelligent enough to continue learning from its human interactions as well as updates to the law.

While not as ubiquitous as Lexis and Westlaw are in large law firms, ROSS can already count several of the largest firms as clients. Additionally, Andrew Arruda, co-founder of ROSS, has been quoted as saying, "We want ROSS to be on the legal team of every lawyer in the world."[9] This technology will certainly change the way lawyers and legal researchers go about their work. Instead of mining a vast list of results, these professionals would be much more efficient and able to focus on higher-level work that is more valuable to their clients. Given the technology and the enthusiasm of leadership, it appears ROSS will be shaking things up in the legal space for years to come.

Casetext (CARA)

Casetext launched CARA in June 2016. In a short time, the company has made a name for itself with several AmLaw 200 firms subscribing to the software. This is because CARA has revolutionized the way researchers identify relevant case law. CARA employs AI technology alongside advanced data science concepts to link users to pertinent content. The user simply drops a brief into the system and CARA provides the user with applicable case law to help bolster the arguments presented in the filing. In discussing how CARA works with Anand Upadhye, VP of business development for Casetext, he stated, "We started with a system that processes the corpus of U.S. common law using statistical topic modeling, natural language processing, and semantic analysis, in addition to principles that govern treatment of large data sets."

Recent enhancements to the platform allow users to locate related briefs, which provides users with other perspectives and potentially useful arguments to be included in their own documents. Additionally, CARA's guided search suggests search terms based on the content of the brief uploaded. This means users do not have to think about the appropriate terms for their search. Furthermore, this feature is based on terms extracted through a self-optimizing algorithm, which means users can feel confident they are always receiving valid recommendations. CARA allows users to do research efficiently and effortlessly. With an eye toward innovation and additional funding,[10] future enhancements to the platform are sure to be notable.

Conclusion

Applications of AI in legal research databases are resulting in powerful and intuitive platforms that are changing the way researchers approach their work. While research platforms like Lexis and Westlaw are not getting rid of Boolean searching, we are beginning to see a shift from the strict rules power users have respected for so long when conducting legal research. The ability to enter or speak a question into a system or to simply drop and drag a document into a tool and be provide with an answer or valuable information is unmatched. There is no doubt that AI and changes to user interfaces will continue to make platforms better and make researchers more efficient. The future of legal research platforms looks bright, but attorneys and legal researchers do not have to worry that they will be replaced with robots...yet.

References

1. Ease! The Compact, Friendly Terminal that Simplifies Legal Research, *ABA Journal 69 (January 1983), 11* Retrieved from https://books.google.com
2. *WestSearch: WestlawNext Search Technology*, Westlaw Next Quick Reference Guide (2011), See: http://west.thomson.com/documentation/westlaw/wlawdoc/web/wlnwsrch.pdf.
3. Wheeler, Ronald E., "Does WestlawNext Really Change Everything: The Implications of WestlawNext on Legal Research", *Law Library Journal*, Vol. 103, No. 3, p. 359, 2011; Univ. of San Francisco Law Research Paper No. 2011-09. See: https://ssrn.com/abstract=1773767
4. *Westlaw Enhancements* See: http://legalsolutions.thomsonreuters.com/law-products/westlaw-legal-research/enhancements
5. LexisNexis Newsroom. (2015). *LexisNexis Acquires Premier Legal Analytics® Provider Lex Machina* [Press Release] See: https://www.lexisnexis.com/en-us/about-us/media/press-release.page?id=1448052993491885&y=2015
6. LexisNexis Newsroom. (2017). *LexisNexis Announces Acquisition of Ravel Law* [Press Release] See: https://www.lexisnexis.com/en-us/about-us/media/press-release.page?id=1496247082681222&y=2017
7. Engagdet. (2011, January 13). *IBM's Watson Supercomputer Destroys Humans in Jeopardy* [Video File]. See: https://youtu.be/WFR3lOm_xhE
8. http://www.rossintelligence.com/
9. *Andrew Arruda of ROSS Intelligence: "We Want to Assist Every Lawyer in the World"*
10. Johnson, Khari "Casetext raises $12 million for legal research assistant CARA" (March 22, 2017). VentureBeat. See: https://venturebeat.com/2017/03/22/casetext-raises-12-million-for-legal-research-assistant-cara/

Chapter 9:
The evolving online legal research landscape

By Marcia Burris research and information services consultant at HBR Consulting

Recent years have seen accelerating change within law firms, driven by market pressures affecting both firms and their clients. The pressures facing law firms are multi-faceted, and include external pressure from clients to improve value and control legal costs, internal pressures to maintain or improve profitability while adding efficiency, and the need not only to maintain technical competency in the practice of law but also to adopt innovative approaches to enhance value provided to clients and to support the firm's needs. Similar changes have also affected law firm libraries and information departments, which are evolving to better meet the business needs of their firms while supporting the changing research styles of attorneys and other internal clients seeking to interact with information resources in new ways.

Controlling spend and value

Within the past decade, the increasing expectation that corporate law departments control legal spend on behalf of their organizations has led to closer scrutiny of outside counsel costs and calls for change in legal practice. The now well-known ACC Value Challenge, first issued in 2009 by the Association of Corporate Counsel, called for better alignment between the cost and value of legal services provided by law firms, and significantly also called for improvement in efficiency and outcomes. Law firms have responded to the challenge, exploring new approaches to pricing and introducing new project management approaches to handle matters with greater efficiency and consistency.

While the dialogue between law departments and law firms continues, many law departments are also finding savings by taking work in-house to control legal costs. As noted in HBR's Annual Law Department Survey, outside counsel spending has declined as a percentage of total legal spend, accounting for 52 percent of law departments' total spend in 2016, down from the 55 percent reported in the 2015 survey. At the same time, law departments report increased investment in internal resources, including adding legal staff and technology to support added efficiency.[1]

With the need for efficiency underscored by increased competition for client work, law firms have likewise invested in new approaches to strengthen their value proposition, including the adoption of technologies to support the practice and delivery of legal services. Firms are embracing efficiency-enabling measures and adopting technology supporting knowledge management, data analytics, pricing, and legal project management, and some firms are also taking innovative steps to package their work product in new ways to meet client needs.

As firms have grown more sophisticated in their use of technology to leverage their own work product, they have also become increasingly savvy consumers of information resources. Firms today expect to receive high value from their information resource investments, including robust content and features and an ability to leverage data and analytics to inform both business decisions and legal strategy. In addition, they expect to achieve value through high utilization of the resources they purchase, and many law firm libraries have invested in third-party tools such as OneLog and ResearchMonitor to provide usage data beyond what is available directly from information vendors, enabling careful management of online subscriptions to optimize usage.

A key aspect of the value proposition is cost, and while firms expect high-quality, innovative features and functionality from their research tools, they are also looking closely at the price of those investments. As law firms strive to provide better value to clients they must also control their own overhead, and in turn they have been looking to their content and technology providers to deliver better value. Research contracts which 10 or 20 years ago might have been accepted as necessary costs of doing business are no longer taken for granted, as both law departments and law firms increasingly adopt "zero-based" budgeting in which each expense must be justified.

As with the ACC Value Challenge, the conversation between law firms and legal information vendors is not exclusively about cost, but rather about the right tools at the right price. What constitutes the right price is being reassessed by many firms, and vendors whose pricing models support the evolving needs of their customers – in addition to providing the high quality resources demanded by users – will see more success in retaining market share than those who do not evolve to meet today's business needs.

Disruptors in the market

While the current business climate sets an often-challenging standard for value, the legal industry's appetite for efficiency-enabling technology has created opportunity for new entrants to gain traction in the legal information market. As law firms demand products enabling high value research outputs, efficient workflows and cost-effectiveness, advances in technology, and increased access to primary law data have empowered a new generation of legal research resources, leading to what seems today to be an ever-growing number of technology and research providers entering the legal information market. Some of these newer platforms offer reduced costs compared to traditional resources, while others tout increased efficiency, or both. Many new products promise to leverage analytics or apply algorithms in new ways to enable faster, more accurate, or easier-to-digest research results. Platforms increasingly feature mapping, color coding, and other visual aids to enhance comprehension and speed research. Established vendors similarly continue to enhance their platforms though new search interfaces and analytics offerings leveraging advanced technology, as well as expanding their secondary content offering through strategic development and acquisitions, as they each strive to be the "best in class" resource for their market.

Ongoing user demand for enhanced functionality will continue to spur product development by both established and new vendors, with an emphasis on search, analytics, and features enabling users to interact with data in news ways. AI products are of high interest, with new applications utilizing AI for improved data mining for business intelligence, in predictive analytics, and in transactional applications, as well as in enhanced research delivery.[2] While AI is a broad term and applies to a number of advanced technologies which can be leveraged for more efficient problem solving, in the research area these applications often feature natural language understanding, image pattern recognition, machine learning, and inference. AI applications, similar to prior technology advances which have already matured, hold the promise of ever more efficient workflows and an ability to digest and analyze vast amounts of data exceeding human capabilities. As firms continue their efforts to increase efficiency vendor innovation in AI, research analytics, and visualization tools will be rewarded in the market. While these products are already gaining market share, HBR's 2016 Law Firm Library Survey showed that firms are planning additional future investment in these product categories.[3]

Content sourcing strategies

As provider options multiply, firms must make strategic decisions regarding content sourcing. A top trend of interest to the law library community is the discontinuation by law firms of one of the traditionally predominant legal research providers, Westlaw or Lexis, sometimes referred to as going "sole provider". While historically it was expected that most large firms would maintain subscriptions to both providers, recently we have seen more firms cut back in this area by cancelling one of the major providers. While this movement away from maintaining both traditional platforms has been at times assessed as affecting primarily small to mid-sized firms, recently we have seen more large firms take this step, including firms in the AmLaw 100 and 200, with the trend more visible among "second hundred" firms. HBR's 2016 Law Firm Library Survey[4] found that 40 percent of respondents had selected a single major provider for online research and cancelled either Westlaw or Lexis. Among firms which had not yet made that change, 60 percent were considering doing so, and although many did not have a timeline in place, 40 percent of that group indicated they were contemplating such a change in the next 1–3 years. While the percentage of survey respondents that indicated they had selected a single primary provider was higher than in HBR's experience working with clients, we do see this as an area to continue to watch, and a likely ongoing trend in light of the other market factors at play.

For firms contemplating the cancellation of a major research provider, cost reduction is often the starting point in deliberations, but is by no means the prime consideration. Firms seeking to position their practices for the future are looking for value and return on investment, which may not always come from selecting the lowest cost approach.

While specific needs and priorities vary among firms, key factors in content selection decisions typically include:

- User experience and attorney preference;
- Access to unique "must-have" content to support a specific practice;
- Value, as defined by firm-specific needs and often driven by secondary content and features;
- Integration with other resources used by the firm; and
- Cost.

In addition to considerations regarding content, functionality, and cost of specific research products, firm decisions regarding potential changes in research service subscriptions are significantly influenced by the organization's internal goals and culture. A key factor in a decision to cut back on a major resource is whether the firm's philosophy encompasses providing multiple options to support individual attorney preferences, or prioritizes a more unified approach in which the firm consolidates its investment in fewer resources. While the opportunity for each user to select the resources they prefer allows firms to meet a variety of user wants and needs, this approach also can contribute to a landscape of multiple under-utilized resources, as well as higher costs and potential information overload or resource confusion as attorneys seek the best resource for a specific information need.

Another important consideration is the firm's position on cost recovery. While a firm's decision regarding whether to charge clients for online research obviously impacts client relationships and the firm's revenue stream, it also strongly affects associate attitudes toward research. A policy of billing online research costs can in some instances lead researchers to avoid tools the firm has invested in, instead relying on free alternatives rather than incur costs which might be questioned by partners or clients. Even when the firm's paid subscriptions are used, the user's approach may emphasize cost avoidance strategies rather than focusing on effective, efficient workflows and successful results.

Many firms opting to consolidate research onto a primary platform plan the timing of the change to coincide with a change in their online billing practices, such as moving away from cost recovery or designating a specific "free" resource for client work. In these scenarios, savings from cancellation of a costly research platform can offset any revenue loss from discontinuing cost recovery across platforms. At the same time, offering users a "no charge" alternative prior to cancelling an existing provider can help drive usage to the new preferred resource by providing attorneys a strong incentive to utilize the service.

Regardless of the firm's decision regarding cost recovery, cancelling an expensive research subscription creates opportunity to invest in new technologies and resources, enabling firms to optimize their mix of research services to meet their future practice needs. We anticipate this trend will continue, with more dialogue and openness to change among the largest firms over the next few years.

Vendor innovation

As the major vendors contemplate greater competition within a narrowing market, they have adopted strategies to make themselves indispensable to their customers. In addition to incorporating advanced technology to enhance the search and analytics features of their platforms, we have also seen a trend of vendors acquiring highly valued and exclusive secondary content. This content is then incorporated into integrated platforms which enable users to discover relevant results from a variety of proprietary resources within the vendor's expanded collection of content. While these highly-integrated search platforms provide an enhanced user experience, the trend toward more integrated content has been accompanied by related changes in vendor pricing structures. The pricing models and content segment options available to subscribers have become more structured and in many instances reduced to a smaller set of simplified options, making it difficult for firms to pick and choose specific content to match their needs and pushing firms toward purchasing bundled content under an "all or nothing" model. While firms can often benefit from broadly inclusive subscriptions, the higher levels of access and higher costs are not always the best fit for a firms' specific needs. In some instances, firms which would otherwise purchase their preferred content from a leading provider find themselves seeking alternative sources rather than pay for bundled content that they do not need. The alternatives firms turn to vary, and can range from purchasing similar secondary content from another source, to reordering print sets that might have been canceled in the past as users migrated to using materials online. Certainly in the area of content structure and subscription pricing, the dialogue between vendors and their law firm customers will need to continue, to ensure value is achieved on both sides.

The influx of new legal information providers and evolving content and subscription options from established providers pose considerable challenges for buyers of information resources. In a trend noted by law librarians as well as other industry observers, many firms today find it helpful to engage outside perspective to support their decision processes regarding online research sources. While many firms first utilized consultants to identify cost saving opportunities or renegotiate contracts during the financial crisis period of 2007-2009 and in subsequent years, firms have increasingly recognized the value of engaging industry experts to provide market intelligence and strategic insights to support their efforts to optimize content mix and costs to meet firm needs. Cost management remains important, but the conversation has expanded to include more strategic assessment of information resources to best support attorneys' needs, with a central goal of positioning the firm for the future.

A successful review of resources includes evaluation of internal and external data, qualitative assessment, and an understanding of the firm's current state, as well as a vision for the future. The consulting project may include various elements, but common steps include:

- Discussion of firm goals and culture;
- Assessment of firm needs, including specific practice and attorney requirements;
- Review of current content utilization, including primary and secondary resources, as well as mapping of similar content across vendor platforms and content gap analysis;
- Assessment of platform preference and user reasons for preference, incorporating analysis of user roles and openness to change in addition to prior usage trends;
- Evaluation of available resource options including current and potential suppliers, with recommendations based on the consultant's access to broader market information; and
- Negotiation with vendors on behalf of the client, or supplying strategy for the client to implement on their own.

The ultimate goal of modern consultative relationships in the library and research space is to help firms achieve a strategic, forward-looking approach to vendor alignment, delivering optimal resources to attorneys at an appropriate cost. Given the significant recent growth in this area, it seems apparent that many firms find having relationships with consultants to be beneficial to the value proposition.

The legal information resource market continues to evolve, with new technology, new providers, and new practice needs to consider now and going forward. These ongoing changes in the legal information resource landscape create opportunity for firms to reassess, realign, and optimize their resources for the future. Doing so will position firms to meet their attorneys' – and their clients' – expectations for years to come.

References

1. HBR Consulting, "2016 Law Department Survey," 2016 See: http://www.hbrconsulting.com/law-department-survey/
2. HBR Consulting, "Artificial Intelligence: Innovation in the Legal Profession", 2017 See: http://www.hbrconsulting.com/insights/ai-innovation/
3. HBR Consulting, "2016 Evolving Libraries Survey for Law Firms", 2016 See: http://www.hbrconsulting.com/wp-content/uploads/2017/02/Evolving-Libraries-Executive-Summary.pdf
4. See note 1, above